D0660034

Thinking and Acting
Together

Thinking and Acting Together

God's Guidance of the Corporate Life
of the Church through the
First Seventy-Five Years of the Work of the
General Assembly of the Church of God

Compiled and Edited by
Barry L. Callen

**The Executive Council
of the Church of God
and
Warner Press, Inc.
Anderson, Indiana**

Arlo F. Newell, Editor in Chief
Dan Harman, Book Editor
Cover by David Liverett

TABLE OF CONTENTS

Foreword

The Executive Council of the Church of God is grateful for the opportunity to join Warner Press in this presentation to the General Assembly on its seventy-fifth anniversary year. Thinking and acting together comes at considerable cost and is often filled with tension and anxiety. This book is compiled to help bring together, in one volume, the directions we have accepted with the leadership of the Holy Spirit.

The Church of God, though loosely structured, has modeled a method of working together which has proven effective. Though we value our liberty, we voluntarily surrender ourselves to an accountability to one another. That commitment to our brothers and sisters in the faith makes possible an effective and dynamic cooperation.

I salute the General Assembly for its wise and redemptive pronouncements and its selection of leadership. I salute, also, the contribution of Barry Callen in making available to those present this year, 1992, a copy of our history across these seventy-five years of the assembly's life. I further salute Warner Press for its contribution of expertise, time, and money to help the Executive Council fund this helpful review of our life together.

Edward L. Foggs
Executive Secretary
Executive Council of the Church of God

Preface

Most Christian fellowships establish a pattern of formal church authority which defines accepted doctrines and regulates group life. Sometimes the power centers in a pope or council of bishops, sometimes in synods, conferences, or superintendents. Such centralizing of ecclesiastical prerogative is justified either by claiming that God established things that way in the church or by assuming that practical necessity left no option.

This typical pattern, however, has been resisted for over a century by a reformation movement known simply as the Church of God. From its beginning in about 1880 this movement has longed to return to the truths, simplicities and Spirit-directedness of the apostolic church. This longing has resulted in an unwillingness to accept and perpetuate the centuries of corruption and humanization that have burdened the life of the Christian community. In the face of a maze of brittle and binding church creeds and complex and coercive church organizations, this movement has attempted to remain open to the fresh and freeing moves of the Spirit of God. While much of traditional church life has tended to function in mechanical and manipulative ways more related to the non-church world than to what the New Testament teaches, there has been a persistent determination in this movement of the Church of God: Such will not be so among us!

Once only a vision burning in the hearts of a few, this movement of the Church of God now has emerged as a worldwide phenomenon with organized programming of gospel proclamation, education, and service. Ministers, initially isolated from one another, found themselves desiring fellowship, inspiration, and a coordination of activity, so assemblies of leaders developed and came to assume a business as well as a strictly spiritual nature.

By 1917 the most prominent of these assemblies was meeting annually in Anderson, Indiana. Since then this assembly has formalized its identity and functions, created the Executive Council as its legal arm and, while remaining a voluntary body, has become very influential in the oversight of most of the movement's cooperative ministries which are based in the United States. This oversight is accomplished through the allocation of funds raised nationally for cooperative ministries, the election of trustees who govern church agency corporations and the ratification of the chief executive officers of these corporations. Oversight also is accomplished by the influence of the assembly's united voice when a consensus can be reached on issues of common concern.

Through the years this General Assembly has sought to be careful to avoid "exercising ecclesiastical authority" in the process of its work. After all, it is not the church sitting in control of local church congregations; nor is it the board with legislative power over the several boards that direct the work of the national corporations. Being the most representative body of the movement, however, on many occasions the General Assembly has spoken its corporate opinion and even expectation to Church of God

1

congregations, the national agencies, and the church and society at large. It has announced convictions and sounded warnings. It has attempted to encourage vision, influence opinion, gather resources, and mobilize effort. While abhorring the very idea of organizing and controlling the church itself, God's family, it certainly has sought to coordinate, direct, and energize the work of the church. The challenge has been to be active and effective in common ministry and mission without being guilty of manipulating and denominationalizing the life of the church.

The following pages describe this General Assembly of the Church of God. They tell of its origin, nature, role, and constitution. They record many of its more significant actions taken and opinions expressed over the decades up to this, its seventy-fifth year of service. They also include some central questions that must find answers as the General Assembly faces the future, still determined to be faithful to the call of God while never assuming the place of God in the church.

As compiler and editor, my intent has not been to increase the General Assembly's power or fame, things it never has desired. Rather, the goal has been to make available significant material in convenient form. Crises have been faced, victories have been won, convictions have been voiced—God has been at work! All of this deserves to be made available for the guidance of generations to come.

The organization of the materials is designed for the convenience of the reader who is wanting either a general overview of the General Assembly and its work or easy access to materials on a given subject.

Barry L. Callen
Anderson, Indiana
June, 1992

Section I

General Assembly: Introduction

A. The Setting

1. Functioning above Sectarianism

by Leslie W. Ratzlaff

Editor's note: The following provides theological perspective on the nature of local Christian congregations as traditionally perceived among Church of God people. Congregations relate voluntarily to the reformation movement and to any agencies or assemblies formed to assist with the work of the church.

Excerpted from an article by Leslie W. Ratzlaff in *Vital Christianity*, 30 June 1985, 22.

Sectarian chains bind God's people, mar their work, and keep the Church from reflecting God's full glory. To forever throw off sectarian cords takes eternal vigilance. The following points suggest transcending and rising above all sectarian cords:

1. The Church of God transcends any human beginning! God gave it birth on the Day of Pentecost as attested to in Acts 2. The year 1881 may be a year when bold action based on discoveries about the Church of God was taken. It, however, was not the beginning but the affirmation of a reality in existence.

2. The Church of God belongs simply to the triune God! To be other than the Church of God "from whom every family in heaven and on earth is named" (Eph. 3:15) is sectarian and to be called other than that presents a confusing witness.

3. The Church of God transcends any human geographical center! God's headquarters are not in Jerusalem (John 4:20-24) and certainly not in Anderson, Indiana. Yet each local congregation is planted in a specific geographical area and should be so identified.

4. The Church of God transcends any reformation movement! Paul took a firm stand against the tendency to sectarian spirit (1 Cor. 1:10-13; 3:1-9). God uses human agents but only God is to be exalted and glorified. The Church of God is greater than any reformation movement. Neither does it exist to serve the reformation movement. Rather the movement exists to serve the church.

5. The Church of God with its biblical base honors and incorporates into its life-style all truth. It is greater than any or all of them; therefore, to call it baptist, pentecostal, presbyterian, or any of a host of other names restricts the church, its witness and its commitment to Christian unity.

6. The Church of God transcends any human alliance! Alliance separates from fellow Christians. Cooperation, yes; formal alliances, no. The Church of God is married to Christ alone and responds ultimately only to the Divine drumbeat.

In summary let it be understood that the Church of God reformation movement along with other reforming movements is an important servant of Christendom. Its task is to help the Church awaken and constantly measure up to God's standard. It plays a John-the-Baptist role in helping the Church come into God's own. The reformation movement serves to provide agencies that help the Church fulfill her Kingdom-building assignment.

The local Church of God congregation, however, is under the sovereignty of God and is a divine-human organism answerable to God alone. Its relationship to the Church of God reformation movement is voluntary.

B. The Nature

2. Parallel to a Local Church Business Meeting

by Russell R. Byrum

Excerpted from the 1992 *Yearbook of the Church of God*, (Anderson, Indiana), 6.

The General Ministerial Assembly of the Church of God is the ministers of the church at the International Camp Meeting assembled in business session. The General Ministerial Assembly is for the purpose of giving general direction to the business and to the various business agencies of the church in general. It sustains practically the same relation to the general church that a business session of a local congregation sustains to the local church. As the local church assembled in business session discusses and determines its business policies in a general way, and appoints financial officers, trustees, or other business agencies for the accomplishment of its work, so the General Ministerial Assembly discusses and determines in a general way what general business interests the church shall conduct and appoints certain men to be responsible for the carrying out of certain business policies. For example, it elects the twenty-four members of the Gospel Trumpet Company, the members of the Church Extension Board, and the registrar of the Clergy Bureau.

It is also parallel with the local church business meeting in that it has no power to determine standards of doctrine or practice, to confer ministerial authority upon any one, to appoint ministers to particular fields, or to do any other thing that is properly the work of the Holy Spirit in his church.

Its officers consist of a chairman and a secretary and it is organized under constitution and bylaws according to common parliamentary practice. Only ordained ministers have the franchise.

C. The Origin

3. A Modest Beginning Motivated by Need

by Marvin J. Hartman

Excerpted from a thesis submitted to the School of Religion of Butler University, Indianapolis, Indiana, 1958.

Much of the information concerning the background of the General Ministerial Assembly has been lost in the history of the movement. Because of the fact that there was no organization, much of the discussion that took place in the early ministers' meetings was never written down. Indeed there seems to have been an aversion to writing deliberations down. One wonders if this was not done because it may have been an indication and an admission that there was not full and strong unity. It must have been frustrating for those who believed so strongly in the unity of the saints to have to admit that the saints did not always agree.

Although it was not until 1917 that the General Ministerial Assembly officially organized, there were, prior to that time, what were called "general assemblies." These seemed to have a pattern across the church of taking place whenever a group of ministers got together to discuss their work. As early as 1902, at Yellow Lake, Indiana, this happened. Charles E. Brown reports:

The first Assembly that I remember attending took place at the Yellow Lake Camp Meeting in 1902. The ministers present at the camp meeting assembled in the men's dormitory and sat around on the beds and talked. The only touch of a formal organization in this meeting was the appointment by this informal gathering of one man to represent the group in talking to the railroads concerning the availability of clergy rates.[1]

Dr. Brown suggests that 1917 is only the formalizing date of an already existing organization. As early as 1906, there was always held—in connection with the Anderson Camp Meeting—a general assembly. This, indeed, was like the other general assemblies that took place whenever ministers got together. The main interest in these general assemblies was preaching. Influential ministers would exhort and encourage the brethren along the lines of the true doctrine. Sometimes in these early assemblies a discussion would take place. The discussion generally would go far enough along so as to start to draw various differences of opinions. Frequently, at this point "one of the more influential brethren would stand and say, 'Now, brethren, this is the way we believe the question.' "[2]

Evidence of the significant role played by the Gospel Trumpet Company is seen in the very first meeting of the temporary organization of the assembly which was held on June 14, 1917. At this meeting, the Gospel Trumpet Company submitted a slate of nominees for company membership. This was significant, because prior to this time the company membership was chosen in a self-perpetuating manner. This change was a wise

6

move. It gave the ministry a feeling of participation, and set a precedent, both legal and moral, for future organizations tied legally with the assembly, to have their membership likewise elected by the assembly. Although the voting was done by yes and no votes on a slate of twenty-four men, there was remarkable unity at this first thrust of responsibility.

The other modest business taken care of in that first General Ministerial Assembly meeting is shown in the following items listed from the minutes of that first meeting [June 14, 1917]:

A motion was made that in the temporary organization only ordained ministers of the Church of God have the right to vote. Motion seconded. Motion carried.

Motion was made and seconded that all ordained ministers of the Church of God in the congregation be requested to rise and stand for purposes of identification. Motion carried.

A motion was made and seconded that a majority of votes of the Assembly shall be sufficient for election to any office for which the Assembly may hold election. Motion carried.

Motion that voting and elections be by ballot. Motion seconded. Motion carried.

Motion that members of the Gospel Trumpet Company who are ordained ministers have a right to vote in this Assembly. Motion seconded. Motion carried.

Motion moved and seconded that the chair appoint a committee of five to draft a constitution and a permanent set of bylaws to govern the Assembly. Motion carried. (J. W. Phelps, A. B. Frost, H. A. Sherwood, O. E. Line, R. R. Byrum—these names were written in pen, in long-hand, in the minutes, with the two words after their names—"were appointed.").

Temporary organization was effected by nominating R. L. Berry, A. T. Rowe, and E. A. Reardon as chairmen pro tem. E. A. Reardon was elected.

Since the Anderson Camp Meeting in these early days was ten days long, the committee to draft the constitution and bylaws had time to work on that task. Evidently for this reason there were no other meetings of the Assembly for a week. Then on June 21 the report of the committee on the constitution was read and approved.

The *Gospel Trumpet* gave considerable space to comment on the 1917 General Ministerial Assembly. It, no doubt, was concerned with reaffirming in the minds of the ministers who were there the wisdom of this step, and also in communicating to those who were not there exactly what happened. There would always be a danger that some of those who were against organization might misrepresent or misquote to those who were not there. Therefore, the brethren were prompted to give considerable space to this 1917 historical meeting.

Indeed, while the meeting was going on, the *Trumpet* said in the June 28 issue (no doubt written a week prior to its publication), the following:

All things of the meeting have been marked by a sweet spirit of

7

unity that is most convincing to those who visit these camp grounds that God is truly in our midst.

The business interests of the church are receiving more careful attention than ever before. The Lord has given the ministry a larger vision of our unparalleled opportunities for spreading the pure gospel to the end of the earth. A deep desire is manifested to see a great forward movement along lines of activity and gospel work—both in the homeland and in the foreign fields. Our vision is not localized, but worldwide in its scope and purpose. In order to insure a sound financial basis for these increased activities, better business methods are being considered for the future than we have been accustomed to in the past.

It has also been felt for some time that there should be a more direct legal relationship existing between the publishing work and the general body of the ministry. Steps have been taken to place this great work in more immediate touch with the ministry, and thereby increase their responsibility for and their interest in this important phase of gospel work. New members have been added to the Gospel Trumpet Company, increasing the number to twenty-four. These twenty-four names were ratified by a vote of the ministers in session at the present camp meeting.

The motivating drive and power which characterized all the development of the organizational machinery of the General Ministerial Assembly seemed to be one of "need." To do the work of God, the early leaders discovered they had to "render unto Caesar" in some areas. The government—local, state, and national—made certain requirements regarding corporations, holding real and personal property, and so forth. The railroad needed a sponsoring national agency to clear membership of clergy for discount in rail travel. The boards and agencies were forced to comply with certain restrictions, which in turn affected the assembly. In short, the General Ministerial Assembly found it could not do the work of the Lord unorganized in a highly organized society. Many times, as the organizational pattern was developing, the thread-worn (but nonetheless, answer of the hour) phrase, "We can organize the work of the church but not the church," was marshalled in defense of the developing organization at Anderson.

1. Personal interview with Charles E. Brown, October 15, 1957.
2. Brown

8

4. Provision of Guidance to Boards and Agencies

Excerpted from the 1960 *Yearbook of the Church of God*, 12.

The Church of God is composed of many people in many congregations scattered all around the world. The GENERAL MINISTERIAL ASSEMBLY is the most representative body within the Church of God through which its world mission and concern can be expressed unitedly and its worldwide work can be approached cooperatively.

The cooperative worldwide work in the main is carried on by duly authorized boards and agencies serving to help all our churches do together what they could never accomplish separately. Through the GENERAL MINISTERIAL ASSEMBLY, our worldwide agencies are set up, and to them was delegated responsibility for particular areas of cooperative work.

The GENERAL MINISTERIAL ASSEMBLY gives direction and guidance to these boards and agencies in the following five ways:

1. Establishment of Policies. Through charters, articles of incorporation, constitutions, and bylaws, the GENERAL MINISTERIAL ASSEMBLY defines the areas of work of the particular agency, its scope of activities, its power, duties, and limitations.

2. Elections. The ASSEMBLY delegates authority for action in particular areas of its work through the election of responsible persons to serve on its boards and agencies. Through these elections to duly authorized boards, work in particular assigned areas of the church's concern can be carried on effectively.

3. Ratifications. Through periodic ratification of the chief executive of each board or agency, the ASSEMBLY approves the delegation of responsibility to that person. This is done at the beginning of each term of office of that chief executive.

4. The Right of Review. Through annual reports which are required from each board, the ASSEMBLY may review the work of that board periodically. Through its Executive Council the work of that board is coordinated with that of other boards. The ASSEMBLY also on occasion has exercised the right to review the work of the particular board through the appointment of a special committee or commission. Thus the ASSEMBLY may satisfy itself that the work assigned is being carried on in accordance with the established policies of the ASSEMBLY.

5. Adoption of Annual Budget. Through its adoption of the annual budget, the ASSEMBLY continues to support and give guidance to the various areas of work assigned to particular boards and agencies.

9

E. The Constitution

5. Constitutional Guidelines

June 1990

ARTICLE I
Name
The name of this body is the General Assembly of the Church of God (hereinafter referred to in this Constitution and Bylaws as "Assembly") with general offices located in Anderson, Indiana.

ARTICLE II
Purpose
The purpose of this Assembly shall be to function as a temporary presbytery in the conduct of the general business of the Church of God and its annual International Convention. In the continuing fulfillment of this purpose it shall provide for and devise measures to create and maintain a legally incorporated coordinating council (hereinafter referred to as the Executive Council) and such other legally incorporated general agencies and/or boards as shall be necessary to arrange for and promote the work of the Church in its national and international relations.

ARTICLE III
Limitations
This Assembly shall be regarded as a voluntary association. It shall not exercise ecclesiastical jurisdiction or authority over the Church in general or over individual congregations in particular. But it shall, however, retain the right of a voluntary association to define its own membership and to declare, on occasion, when individual ministers or congregations are not recognized by the Assembly as adhering to the general reformation principles to which the Assembly itself is committed.

ARTICLE IV
Membership
The members of this Assembly shall consist of the following persons who are present at any authorized and duly called meeting of the Assembly.

Section 1: Ordained ministers of the Church of God in good and regular standing.

Section 2: Unordained ministers who are pastors or full-time associate pastors of recognized congregations.

Section 3: Laity who are elected or appointed members of the Executive Council, a subordinate board, committee, or commission of the Assembly or the Executive Council.

Section 4: One layperson selected by each recognized state or provinced assembly; a representative selected by each recognized state or provincial organization of WOMEN OF THE CHURCH OF GOD; and a represen-

10

tative selected by each recognized state or provincial organization of the Church of God Men, International.

Editor's note: Articles V-VIII contain detailed guidelines for meetings, amendments to the Constitution, the definition of a quorum, and so on.

F. The Leadership

6. Persons Chosen to Lead

1917 to Date

Joseph T. Wilson	1928-1929	Arlo F. Newell	1968-1974
Charles E. Brown	1929-1931	Leonard W. Snyder	1974-1975
Joseph T. Wilson	1931-1932	Arlo F. Newell	1975-1977
E. E. Perry	1933-1934	Paul L. Hart	1977-1983
Albert F. Gray	1934-1936	Samuel G. Hines	1983-1989
Joseph T. Wilson	1936-1939	Oral Withrow	1989-1990
Albert F. Gray	1939-1954	David Cox	1990-1992
Harold W. Boyer	1954-1968		

Section II

Selected Position/Action Resolutions

A. Organizational Guidelines
B. Identification of *Reformation Principles*
C. Distribution of Resources
D. Christian Higher Education
E. Major Social Issues
F. Emphases, Studies, Celebrations

A. Organizational Guidelines

7. Only Ordained Ministers Can Vote

June 1917

The General Ministerial Assembly passed its first motion in its initial year of formal existence. Because of the long pattern which it established, it is significant to note a motion recorded in the assembly minutes of 14 June 1917.

A motion was made that in the temporary organization only ordained ministers of the Church of God have the right to vote. Motion seconded. Motion carried.

8. Establishment of the Executive Council

June 1932

The Golden Jubilee celebration in 1931 marked a time of historic review and future projections for the reformation movement. One result was the 1930 General Ministerial Assembly authorization of the appointment of a commission on assembly reorganization. The commission's report, which included a plan to make the assembly a delegated body, was rejected by the 1931 assembly, but another action of the 1930 assembly did become reality. It called for the consideration of a "business body" to manage the general interests of the church. In 1932 the assembly altered its bylaws to provide for the creation and incorporation of the Executive Council of the Church of God. The 20 June 1932 minutes read:

The objects and purposes of the corporation are hereby declared to be to promote the religious and benevolent work of the Church of God, and for such purposes such corporation shall have power to receive, take and hold real and personal property, donations of money and property, legacies and bequests, and to sell, transfer and otherwise convey such property, on behalf of the Church of God, to sue and defend any and all actions in any court, and to have, hold and enjoy all the rights, privileges and powers of corporations at common law.

In 1947 the General Ministerial Assembly authorized the Commission on Revision and Planning to study ways for achieving better coordination of the general work of the church. As a result, the 1954 assembly amended the Articles of Incorporation of the Executive Council and in 1956 took even further action by increasing both the membership and responsibilities of the council. According to Article III, Section 1 of the constitution of the General Assembly as revised in June 1980:

The Executive Council shall serve as coordinating council for the Assembly. It shall coordinate the work of the general agencies authorized by the Assembly in their interrelated and cooperative functions, in their promotional and fund-raising activities, and in the services they offer to the Church at large. It shall promote the general welfare and cooperative work of the Church of God.

Then in 1991 the assembly approved a new set of expectations for the council. See entry 113.—Ed.

The following persons have provided significant leadership for the work of the Executive Council (years listed are those of the respective yearbooks where these names appear):

Presidents, Board of Directors		Secretary-Treasurers	
Robert L. Berry	1934-1937	W. Burgess McCreary	1934-1936
Elver F. Adcock	1937-1946	Earl L. Martin	1936-1937
John A. Morrison	1946-1948	Adam W. Miller	1937-1938
William E. Reed	1948-1955	Dale Oldham	1938-1944
Steele C. Smith	1955-1960	I. K. Dawson	1944-1947
Marvin J. Hartman	1961-1965	Lawrence E. Brooks	1947-1955
Carl M. Poe	1966-1970		
Marcus H. Morgan	1970-1981	**Executive Secretaries**	
R. Dale Whalen	1981-1984	Clarence W. Hatch	1955-1960
Betty Lewis	1984-1990	Charles V. Weber	1960-1971
David Lynch	1990-	William E. Reed	1971-1980
		Paul A. Tanner	1980-1988
		Edward L. Foggs	1988-

9. Join the Federal Council of Churches?

June 1944

During the 1940s a wave of criticism rolled through the Church of God. Some felt that all of the organizational and program growth had become dysfunctional, that a few "big boys" were trying to "run things" from Anderson "headquarters," that the national leadership was steering the movement away from its historic commitments.

One focus of this concern was an action of the 1944 General Ministerial Assembly establishing a committee to explore a possible relationship with the Federal Council of Churches. Critics saw the very idea of such exploration as a negation of the movement's understanding of Christian unity. The committee reported in 1946 that "due to the pressure of other duties" it had not yet accomplished its task. A motion to continue the committee was lost (149 yes, 158 no). The chairman stated his opinion that the assembly could not commit the Church of God to membership in the federal council even if it so desired. E. F. Adcock, chairman of the committee, clarified that committing the church to regular membership in the council had not been the intention of the committee. The case was closed.

10. Faith in the Integrity of the National Work

June 1947

In a time of considerable tension and misunderstanding when many ministers in the Church of God were openly distrustful of the integrity of the Anderson-based agencies of the church, the General Ministerial Assembly decided it must speak. In June 1947 it adopted the following:

WHEREAS sixty-seven years ago D. S. Warner and his associates in the faith brought into being a new religious movement conceived by the Holy Spirit and predicated upon the ideal of a pure and undivided church; and

WHEREAS to the promulgation of this ideal these hardy pioneers gave their time, talent, money and very lives, and died in the faith that through their humble instrumentality God was working a great work in the world; and

WHEREAS even in their brief day these pioneers hammered out the beginnings of effective organizational instruments for the publishing of this divine message; and

WHEREAS this Assembly has implemented and added to these instrumentalities as need dictated through the years; and

WHEREAS all through its history this work has been attacked both from without and within, but to no permanent avail, because of the strong foundation upon which our work rests; and

WHEREAS now for two and a half years a new attack has been waged against the work, an attack not upon one front of the work alone, but upon every front—a total attack upon the total program and leadership of the work—bitter and persistent, covering every part of our corporate program: evangelism, publication, home and foreign missions, education, Sunday school and youth; including charges specific and general against persons and groups, covering the grossest evils, such as ministerial apostasy, malfeasance in office, misuse of funds, falsification, fraudulent behavior, wholesale doctrinal defection, and extreme worldliness; and

WHEREAS if in the main these charges were true, our Christian conscience would demand that strong measures be taken to remedy such a situation, but since charges in the main are not true, then the same Christian conscience demands that such charges, false and deliberately made, and persistently circulated, be condemned as grossly unchristian, and that those responsible for such unbecoming conduct make proper amends; and

WHEREAS one year ago this Assembly appointed an Investigating Committee of seven competent and trustworthy brethren with the instruction that they investigate the truthfulness of these charges; and

WHEREAS this committee, at the expense of great labor on their part and at a considerable expenditure of money, have so investigated these charges; Now, therefore, be it

RESOLVED: First, that we hereby reaffirm our faith in and loyalty and dedication to the doctrines, ideals, and objectives which gave birth to the movement; and at the same time we express our confidence in the boards and general agencies which serve the Church at home and abroad under the authority of this General Ministerial Assembly; and

Second, that we emphatically disapprove of the spirit and methods employed in the attacks made upon the general work of the Church as unchristian, unbrotherly, and unfair; which attacks have resulted in division and discord among the ministry and the laity as well; and

Third, that this General Ministerial Assembly go on record as being opposed to this program, and to any program by an individual or group that is calculated to cause division among us and break the worldwide unity that has characterized our movement from the beginning; and

Fourth, that we call upon all those responsible for the program which has caused such confusion and division within the Church forthwith to discontinue all such activities; and this Assembly does hereby entreat with all Christian brotherliness of spirit Brother Earl Slacum and those associated with him in the present agitation to acknowledge their error and to make due amends, so that Christian fellowship may be restored and the unity of the Church be preserved; and

Fifth, that we strongly urge our ministers when faced with problems related to our general work, to handle all such matters through the proper channels in a definitely Christian spirit; and

Sixth, that we recommend to the Indiana Ministerial Assembly and to all other State Ministerial Assemblies where such a program of division may be carried on, if the decision of this General Ministerial Assembly as herein expressed is disregarded, that such disciplinary action be taken as will safeguard and insure the unity of the Church; and

Seventh, that copies of this resolution be mailed to all ministers of the Church of God, and that this action be recorded as a part of the permanent minutes of this Assembly.

11. Anderson Camp Meeting to Be Continued and Housed

June 1960

It was not possible to convene the 1960 Anderson camp meeting because of the collapse of the south end of the tabernacle in which the meeting had been held annually for some forty years. A debate followed concerning the appropriate course to follow.

The final action read:

WHEREAS this Assembly has spoken in clear and unmistakable terms favoring the continuance of the Camp Meeting and the Annual General Ministerial Assembly Meeting at Anderson, Indiana, and

WHEREAS facilities for such meetings must be provided, be it therefore

RESOLVED, That the General Ministerial Assembly does hereby authorize and instruct the Executive Council of the Church of God, its legal entity, to proceed at once to provide the facilities for such Camp Meeting and General Ministerial Assembly by one of the following possibilities:

1. The repair of the present partially existing tabernacle at an engineer's estimated cost of $70,500 plus.
2. The erection of a colorable Stran-Steel building over the present tabernacle floor, meeting the state of Indiana building code . . .
3. Or, some other similar priced construction. Be it further

RESOLVED, That the Division of World Service and the Budget Committee of the Executive Council arrange the necessary financing plan for covering the approved construction costs in cooperation with the Executive Council, be it further

RESOLVED, That authorization for awarding the construction contract be made jointly by the Executive Committee of the Executive Council and the Board of Directors of the Gospel Trumpet Company, [and] be it further

RESOLVED, that this Assembly express its desire on these possibilities by ballot in this meeting today.

Editor's note: In 1961 the site for the present Warner Auditorium was dedicated. The decision for the future had been made.

12. Establishment of a Commission on Social Concerns

June 1964

WHEREAS there is manifest interest in a Commission on Social Concerns in the Church of God, and

WHEREAS the Executive Council has received from different sources requests for the establishment of such a Commission on Social Concerns, and

WHEREAS there is manifest urgency for the careful and prayerful study of ways in which articulate calls may be given to the congregations for them to carefully consider Christian responsibility in the fields of temperance and general welfare, particularly with alcohol problems, gambling, tobacco, pornographic literature; in areas of peace and world order, particularly with military policy and legislation for conscription, disarmament and nuclear weapon control; and in the area of human relations, particularly in race relations, civil liberties, church-state relationships, housing, civic responsibility, and

WHEREAS the Executive Council through its Executive Committee and the National Association of the Church of God (West Middlesex, Pennsylvania) through its appointed standing committee on race relations, have concurred in the call for the establishment of a Commission on Social Concerns, and

WHEREAS in other years this Assembly has appointed committees and commissions with responsibility in the areas of social Christian concerns, therefore, be it

RESOLVED, That the General Ministerial Assembly authorize the establishment of a permanent Commission on Christian Social Concerns responsible to the assembly through the Executive Council, and be it further

RESOLVED, That this Commission on Christian Social Concerns shall be established with the purpose, the general areas of concern, the grant of power and lines of responsibility, the determination of membership, and other similar factors within the limitations described in the recommendation from the Executive Council to the General Ministerial Assembly which is attached to this resolution, and which is dated June 15, 1964.

13. Establishment of a Committee on Christian Unity

June 1965

WHEREAS for several years there has been manifest interest in a Committee on Christian Unity, and

WHEREAS resolutions have come from several state ministerial assemblies to the General Assembly or Executive Council calling for such a committee, and

WHEREAS the All Board Congress and Planning Council expressed deep concern for and the need of such a committee, and

WHEREAS the General Assembly has instructed the Executive Council and its Division of General Service to study the need, structure, and responsibility of such a committee and bring a report to the General Assembly, and

WHEREAS representatives of the Church of God have already been in conversation with the representatives of certain other church groups who have sought to become acquainted with the Church of God, therefore, be it

RESOLVED, That a Committee on Christian Unity be authorized by the General Assembly and responsible to the Assembly through the Executive Council, making annual reports with its concluding report in June 1969. . . .

Editor's note: The life of this committee was extended to 1975 when the General Assembly recast this body as a permanent Commission on Christian Unity because (a) "the need and responsibility for unity and cooperative work among Christians is so strategic to Christian witness and world evangelism" and (b) "the Church of God continues to need a representative group to make contacts, hold conversations, and develop lines of cooperation with other church bodies of similar spirit and concern."

14. Name Change to "General Assembly"

June 1965

In 1958 the General Ministerial Assembly redefined its own membership to include "laymen who are elected or appointed members of the Executive Council, a subordinate Board, committee, or commission of the Assem-

18

bly." Although this was implemented immediately, the inconsistency of such action and the name of the assembly were not addressed until 1965.

The June 1965 action read:

INASMUCH as we now have some seventy-five laymen who are duly elected and authorized members of this Assembly, which in fact, makes this a General Assembly rather than a General Ministerial Assembly, therefore, be it

RESOLVED, That the term "General Assembly" be hereinafter used to designate the title of this Assembly and such changes be reflected in this Constitution and Bylaws and other official papers. Article I—Name reads: "The name of this body is the General Assembly of the Church of God (hereinafter referred to in this Constitution and Bylaws as 'Assembly') with general offices located in Anderson, Indiana." and, be it further

RESOLVED, That Article I, Section 2 of the Bylaws be amended by striking out the words, "Any ordained minister of the Church of God in good and regular standing," and inserting the words, "Any member of this General Assembly," making this part of Section 2 read, "Any member of this General Assembly shall be considered eligible for election or appointment to these offices."

15. Office of Associate Executive Secretary

June 1974

THE EXECUTIVE COUNCIL recommends to the General Assembly that authorization be given for the employment of an associate secretary to serve with the executive secretary in the administration of the council's work on behalf of the Assembly and the Church of God. The Executive Council further recommends:

1. That the office of an associate secretary be filled initially by a carefully selected black person who is to be nominated by the Board of Directors of the Executive Council, but with election by the members of the Executive Council and ratification by the General Assembly in the same manner as is the office of the executive secretary.
2. That the term of office for the proposed associate secretary shall be for five years, beginning January 1, 1975, subject to the Assembly's approval of this recommendation.
3. That the General Assembly grant the Executive Council the privilege of submitting the name of a person to fill this office for ratification prior to the adjournment of its June 18-20, 1974, meeting.
4. That the General Assembly approve the budget for the operation of this office recommended by the Budget Committee and by the Executive Council.
5. That the General Assembly will amend its Bylaws, Article V, Ratification of Offices, by adding sub-paragraph (14) to read: (14) Associate Secretary to the Executive Secretary of the Executive Council.

Editor's note: With the above action was a lengthy description of this new position. The following are two central portions of that description:

The associate secretary is to join with the executive secretary in interpreting the policies and decisions of the General Assembly and the Executive Council to other agencies of the Church of God and to any person or groups needing such information. In turn, he is to interpret to the Executive Council and the General Assembly his readings of what is happening on the field and recommend procedures for the strengthening of understanding and cooperation.

The associate secretary is to serve in a liaison relationship between the Executive Council and the black membership of the Church of God. His special assignment will be that of trying to bring about closer ties and relationships within the Church. He shall be responsible to keep the Executive Council, its Board of Directors and the executive secretary fully aware of the needs, feelings, and developments in the black church.

16. Cooperation in Missionary Work

June 1975

The 1974 General Assembly authorized the appointment of a twelve-member committee to:
1. Study the work and impact of the several "mission groups" at work in the Church of God;
2. Study their relationships with the duly constituted national agencies of the Church of God;
3. Study the implications of their promotional efforts on the total programming and fund raising for the agencies authorized by the General Assembly, state assemblies, and other national assemblies.

The report of this committee, presented to and adopted by the 1975 General Assembly, included these recommendations:
1. We recommend that the Executive Council of the Church of God study the feasibility of inviting each of the following organizations now serving the interests of the Church of God to appoint an observer to attend and participate in the annual meeting of the council when budgeting is done for the general work of the church:
—Project Partner with Christ
—Vacation Samaritans
—Men of the Church of God
    The purpose of this recommendation is twofold:
    (1) To provide opportunity for a para-mission organization to receive current information on programmatic and budgetary decisions reached by the Executive Council;
    (2) To provide opportunity for the Executive Council to receive current information on the operations and activities of para-mission groups and to give counsel on how coordination can best be achieved.

20

2. We recommend that the following groups set up a regular schedule of meetings to review planning and coordination of programmatic concerns:
   —The Missionary Board of the Church of God
   —The Board of Church Extension and Home Missions
   —Project Partner with Christ
   —Vacation Samaritans
   —WOMEN OF THE CHURCH OF GOD
   —Men of the Church of God
   The executive secretary of the Executive Council will convene the initial meeting of this group.
3. We recommend that the para-mission organizations which solicit their financial support from the general body of the Church of God congregations and members in the United States report on a yearly basis their financial operations. In implementing this recommendation, it is requested that a copy of the annual Statement of Financial Condition be filed with the office of the executive secretary of the Executive Council for placement in the files of the General Assembly and its Executive Council.
4. We recommend that para-mission organizations, which receive their primary support from the Church of God as represented by the General Assembly and its Executive Council, always consider themselves to be morally and ethically related to the Church of God and follow the practice of selecting a majority of persons of Church of God membership to serve on their Board of Directors and in their corporation membership.
5. We recommend that each para-mission organization, which receives its primary support from Church of God congregations and members, include in its Articles of Association and Bylaws a provision whereby—in case of dissolution—the assets of the corporation will be retained for the benefit of the Church of God and not inure to the benefit of any private persons.

17. Increasing the Participation of Laypersons

June 1979

WHEREAS this Assembly has authorized its Committee on Bylaws and Organization to study ways of increasing lay participation in the General Assembly of the Church of God, and

WHEREAS said committee has spent three years in such a study and has developed a suggested "model" for reconstituting the membership of the Assembly to include more laypersons, therefore, be it

RESOLVED, That the committee be instructed to prepare copies of this "model," along with a packet of explanatory materials, to be sent no later than October 1979 to each congregation listed in the current *Yearbook of the Church of God*, and be it further

RESOLVED, That each congregation be asked to discuss this model and to respond to the Bylaws Committee no later than April 1, 1980, on a form provided, and be it further

RESOLVED, That the committee bring to the 1980 assembly specific recommendations for changing the Assembly's Bylaws along the lines suggested by a consensus of responses from the congregations.

Editor's note: The model referred to is that the membership of the General Assembly should be newly defined to include all members of all Church of God congregations who are present at designated meetings of the assembly; from this group a selected number would be identified as voting members to provide a manageable and representative base for decision making; the voting members would include all ministers and laypersons who currently constitute the General Assembly and, in addition, at least one layperson designated by each local congregation.

The Bylaws Committee did bring to the 1980 assembly the results of a congregational survey for the purposes of information and further clarification. No action was requested. The committee brought to the 1981 assembly a review of the history of the question and proposed that "this same model for increasing lay representation in the General Assembly remain before us for continued refinement and discussion and that it be brought before the 1982 General Assembly for a vote." See entry 20.

18. Procedure for Grievances

June 1980

The 1980 General Assembly sessions included criticism directed at a national agency of the church, Anderson College. The criticism had been focused publicly by an "open letter" mailed by a minister to all assembly members just prior to the convening of the assembly. Apart from the substance of the criticism, the attention of the assembly was directed toward affirming more appropriate ways for future grievances to be handled. Thus, the assembly adopted the following resolution as procedural guidance for the future. It should be noted that in the 1985 assembly, in the midst of criticism being directed at another national agency of the church, Warner Press, the assembly's Business Committee reaffirmed this 1980 action, redistributed it to assembly members, and urged that it be honored. In 1989 the Executive Council and General Assembly reaffirmed a modest revision and reissuing of this procedure.

The original resolution read:

The National Agencies of the Church of God are servants of the church and have been brought into being by action of the General Assembly. Each agency is incorporated and governed by a board of trustees duly elected by this Assembly, and answerable to this Assembly.

It is likely that some agency decisions will be unpopular. Members of this Assembly must know that they do have a voice and that their voice will be heard. Therefore, an accepted procedure for sharing differences, grievances, and suggestions is needed. The Business Committee recommends that the biblical basis found in Matthew 18:15-17 be the accepted norm and procedure. The following process shall then be our guide:

I. AGENCY

    a. A letter to the chief executive officer of the agency in question shall be written seeking an answer or solution. If a solution is not easily resolved by mail, an official meeting with the chief executive officer shall be established at the convenience of both parties.

    b. If such a meeting is unsatisfactory, it will then be appropriate to seek a meeting with the elected officers of the corporation, including the chief executive officer, to seek a solution.

    c. If no solution to the problem is found, attempt shall be made to have the larger governing group of the corporation consider the matter.

II. EXECUTIVE COUNCIL

    a. If the above steps to solve the problem with the agency in question have been exhausted, consultation with the Board of Directors of the Executive Council may be sought to see if proper negotiation can be achieved. The Board of Directors may make the concern an agency item for the Executive Council.

III. GENERAL ASSEMBLY

    a. If the concern is not satisfactorily resolved, the grievance may be presented to the General Assembly, through its Business Committee.

    b. If the Business Committee does not agree to make the concern an agenda item, it may be brought to the floor of the Assembly. By a two-thirds vote of the members present it may then be dealt with directly by the Assembly.

Editor's note: The 1989 revised form of this 1980 grievance procedure laid stress on resolving differences with agency administrators and governing boards at the agency level. The General Assembly was referred to as "the body of last resort" only.

19. Maintaining a Responsible Business Committee

June 1981

The established procedures for conducting the business of the General Assembly seemed to some members of the 1980 assembly to be designed to obstruct their full participation. One minister stated with considerable frustration that, while assembly members were urged to follow orderly procedures, some members often found it difficult to get through the proper channels. Therefore, a motion was adopted that called on the Bylaws Committee of the Assembly to take appropriate action in regard to this concern. The specific recommendation was that any item of business be permitted on the assembly floor if a majority of voting members so desired (instead of the two-thirds vote traditionally required). In conflict with this specific recommendation, however, was another action also taken by the 1980 General Assembly. Because of an "open letter" distributed nationally by an assembly member just prior to the 1980 assembly and in the face of widespread questioning of the appropriateness of this means of bringing a concern to the attention of those in positions of responsibility, the assembly approved a policy governing grievance procedures (see entry 18). The first step called for in this procedure was written contact with the chief executive officer of the agency related to the concern in question. The final step in this procedure, should all else fail to bring some resolution of the problem, was a bypassing of the action of the Business Committee of the assembly by a two-thirds vote of assembly members, thus allowing direct action on the floor of the assembly. This grievance procedure also was forwarded to the Bylaws Committee for appropriate action.

The Bylaws Committee saw the conflict in these two actions of the 1980 General Assembly, one calling for movement from two-thirds to a majority and one specifically retaining the two-thirds vote necessary to bring an item of business to the floor when the Business Committee of the assembly has not agreed to make that concern an agenda item. In light of this conflict, in view of the long-standing two-thirds bylaw of the assembly and with the knowledge that the two-thirds guideline is widely accepted as sound parliamentary procedure, the Bylaws Committee recommended to the 1981 assembly that its standing bylaw not be changed. The assembly accepted this recommendation.

20. Lay Representation in the General Assembly

June, 1982

The following was presented to and approved by the 1982 General Assembly.

BACKGROUND

The Bylaws Committee, through its extensive studies, has noted widespread support for some increase of lay representation to the Assembly. The committee has decided to bring a proposal for adoption to the Assembly this year. The committee acknowledges its responsibility to listen carefully to the Church and that its proposals should reflect procedures that enhance the unity we desire. Therefore, this proposal differs from the one given to the Assembly previously. This proposal comes as a result of the committee's desire to achieve Assembly-wide consensus on this question.

PROPOSAL

Therefore, the Bylaws Committee proposes that the Constitution of the General Assembly, Article IV—Membership, Section 4, which now reads:

One layman may be selected by each state (district), or provincial assembly, to attend the General Assembly as an observer.
be changed to read:

One layperson selected by each recognized state or provincial assembly; a representative selected by each recognized state or provincial organization of WOMEN OF THE CHURCH OF GOD; and a representative selected by each recognized state or provincial organization of the Church of God Men, International.

EXPLANATION AND EFFECT

"Recognized" is understood to mean:

(1) State or provincial assemblies which are recognized by the General Assembly of the Church of God through its Division of Church Service;

(2) State or provincial organizations of the WOMEN OF THE CHURCH OF GOD which are recognized by the National Organization of the WOMEN OF THE CHURCH OF GOD;

(3) State or provincial organizations of the Church of God Men, International which are recognized by the National Organization of Church of God Men, International.

The effect of this change is to bring those persons now designated as observers in the Assembly into full membership in the Assembly. In addition this change brings into the life of the Assembly key proven leaders of two of the Church's vital national organizations. Both organizations endorse heartily the possibility of their participation in the Assembly. The likelihood of faithful participation by these persons is good because of their demonstrated concern for the work of the Church and the high percentage of their attendance already in the convention. The potential addition to the Assembly is approximately one-hundred thirty-five persons.

Editor's note: See entry 113 for a 1991 action approving a significant further expansion of lay assembly members beginning in 1993.

21. Ratification Procedures for New Executives

June 1984

WHEREAS the General Assembly prescribes in its bylaws that certain agency executives shall be presented to it for ratification; and

WHEREAS it is appropriate that the General Assembly know the qualifications and central convictions of persons they are asked to ratify; and

WHEREAS the size and setting of the General Assembly do not make it feasible to engage in a lengthy cross-examination style of questioning; and

WHEREAS a board duly elected by the General Assembly has already reviewed the qualifications of, and elected, the person to be ratified; and

WHEREAS the Assembly requires pre-Assembly mailing of information about nominees; therefore be it

RESOLVED, That the corporate agency presenting the name for

ratification state the qualifications, home church, and credentials of their nominee; and be it further

RESOLVED, That the candidate to be ratified share in writing his/her own experiential testimony and spiritual pilgrimage, including a personal statement of doctrinal convictions; and be it further

RESOLVED, That the Executive Council mailing to General Assembly members in May include both of these documents for their advance study and reflection; and be it further

RESOLVED, That should any agency fail to have such materials ready for advance mailing, such information shall be given to the General Assembly, in session, at least one day prior to the ratification vote; and be it finally

RESOLVED, That no person shall be ratified by the General Assembly on the same day that his/her name is presented to the Assembly for ratification.

22. Warner Press: Concerns and Changes

June 1983-1986

During 1981-82 criticism was heard from several sources about various structures and practices of Warner Press. In response, the Publication Board of Warner Press named a Consultation Committee which brought to the 1983 General Assembly a progress report of the early stages of its work. The committee reported that it was studying:

1. The function and purpose of Warner Press in relation to the Church of God;
2. The propriety and sufficiency of the organizational structure of Warner Press regarding the relationship of the president and editor in chief;
3. The latitude and freedom of the editor in chief to pursue and fulfill this defined function;
4. The editorial policy and its manner of determination; and
5. The sufficiency of the present organizational structure for oversight or review of Warner Press (from the General Assembly through the lowest echelon).

The committee promised to report again to the 1984 General Assembly. In that assembly the chair of the Publication Board spoke for the committee, which had already mailed its final report to assembly members. With the support of the officers and Consultation Committee of Warner Press, there was introduced and adopted a resolution from the Winchester, Kentucky, and Pryor, Oklahoma, Pastors' Fellowships. This resolution noted reception of the report of the Consultation Committee, expressed concern that "spiritual considerations be given preeminence over the financial and operational policies of Warner Press," and called on the Publication Board to bring to the 1985 and 1986 general assemblies a full report on the implementation of the changes outlined in the final report of the Consultation Committee.

Prior to the 1985 assembly, in which the president of Warner Press was scheduled for ratification for a new term, renewed criticism was directed toward Warner Press. In its annual meeting in May 1985, the Executive Council heard the grievances and appointed a Special Committee on Warner Press Grievances, comprising persons outside Warner Press, and charged it to report to the 1985 General Assembly prior to the ratification vote on the president of Warner Press.

In the 1985 General Assembly the Publication Board of Warner Press brought its scheduled implementation report, which was followed by the report of the Special Committee on Warner Press Grievances. This latter report spoke specifically to the issues of bonuses, salaries, and the tenure of board members and called for the ratification of the president of Warner Press for an abbreviated two-year term. It was reported that the Publication Board had agreed to implement all of the recommendations made. Consequently, the president's special two-year term was voted.

The Special Committee made an additional and extensive report to the 1986 Assembly. It included a review of the committee's assignment and work, a summary of expressed concerns about the publishing work and a series of recommendations grouped in four areas. They were: the mission and operational philosophy of Warner Press; the renewal and expansion of our publishing ministries; the utilization of income; and restructuring for effective leadership.

23. Limitation of Terms for Board Members

June 1985

For some years it had been the conviction of some members of the General Assembly that the church would be better served if a limitation were placed on the length of time any one person could serve on a governing board of a national agency. In the assembly of 1985 the Bylaws Committee presented a recommended bylaws change which, as amended on the floor to be even more restrictive, was adopted as stated below.

No person shall be nominated for membership on any subordinate Board who has already served as a member of that Board for two consecutive five (5) year terms or ten consecutive years until after a lapse of two years.

In 1986 this limitation was broadened to three consecutive five-year terms for those governing the institutions of higher education. Then in 1990 the maximum of three terms (fifteen years) was applied to all persons affected by the original 1985 action.

24. Inter-Church Cooperation

June 1985

The following resolution was developed and adopted by the Committee on Long Range Planning (April 1985) and approved by the Executive

27

Council of the Church of God (May 1985). It then was presented to members of the 1985 General Assembly for information and guidance.

WHEREAS the Church of God Reformation Movement has historically affirmed the unity of the Body of Christ as expressed in its many forms, yet one; and

WHEREAS the Church of God Reformation Movement for over eighty years has participated in mutually supportive relationships with other communions through its national and state agencies in missionary education, missions education, and ministerial continuing education; and

WHEREAS ministers and laypersons of the Church of God Reformation Movement have been involved in significant ways in local cooperative ministries such as community concerns, leadership training, and evangelism; and

WHEREAS the Commission on Christian Unity of the Church of God in its 1983 Statement of Concern and Guidance on Christian Unity urged the church "to work toward an intentional togetherness to exercise a willed movement toward each other"; and

WHEREAS the 1984 Consultation on Mission and Ministry established as one of its five priority areas of concern that of being the body of Christ with one of its stated goals "to expand ministries through voluntary relationships with Christian groups outside the Church of God Reformation Movement and seek to live out the vision of unity through broader interdependent relationships that serve mutual needs for training, fellowship, and witness"; therefore, be it

RESOLVED, That the Committee on Long Range Planning supports the historical stance of the Church of God Reformation Movement to seek intentional inter-church relationships through which its own ministries are strengthened and enriched and which provide opportunity for the Church of God Reformation Movement to live out its message of Christian unity through enriching the entire Body of Christ; and be it further

RESOLVED, That all Church of God Reformation Movement national, state, and local structures be encouraged to participate in inter-church relationships as a means of expressing our belief in Christian unity and our desire to effect cooperative ministries.

Editor's note: The 1987 General Assembly adopted a resolution calling for the establishment of a special committee to study, document and evaluate the current involvements of general agencies of the Church of God with the National Council of Churches (U.S.A.) and the World Council of Churches. This committee's report was presented and received with appreciation by the 1988 assembly. It excluded discussion of the World Council since no involvement was found except an occasional "observer status." Portions of this report follow.

Summary Perspectives

The study committee is united in its strong conviction that the Church of God must find increasingly effective ways to express its commitment to

28

Christian unity and to fulfill the mission of the church in the world. We are called to make a difference, but we cannot do it alone.

Diversity and interdependence are both facts of contemporary church life. There is considerable and increasing diversity of backgrounds, beliefs, church traditions and priority agendas now seen in Church of God congregations and among Church of God leaders at all levels of church life. Church of God colleges increasingly are being populated by students from other than Church of God congregations. Many Church of God pastors participate actively with local and area inter-church bodies that provide fellowship and/or cooperative ministry opportunities. Often these bodies include a wide spectrum of church traditions, commitments and agendas. Pastors have the freedom to participate as they judge appropriate and sometimes they do in very visible, formal and influential ways. Interdependence among Christian communities appears necessary for the effective accomplishment of some ministry goals. It also appears to be a natural implementation of the burden for Christian unity carried by the Church of God reformation movement.

Church of God general agencies, with major ministry mandates and limited resources in a complex world, also have evidenced need for "outside" ministry relationships and resources. In a very few instances they have developed limited relationships with working units of the National Council of Churches in Christ as a partial means of fulfilling this need. In such instances the agencies have been especially sensitive to public allegations made against the Council and they have walked carefully the narrow path of restricted involvement designed only to enrich their own work and witness without formal membership or direct involvement in the larger life of the Council itself.

Admittedly there are risks in all sharing relationships; but the isolationist alternative would be a denominationalizing of the Church of God reformation movement—an alternative which inevitably would bring its own high price. Given the risks associated with all alternatives, then, the study committee seemed to face a choice between (a) calling for a blanket prohibition of all such participation with working units of the NCCC or similar inter-church bodies and (b) calling for no action, thus leaving the general agencies free to relate to whom and as they see fit. The committee judged neither of these choices acceptable. Rather, the committee saw wisdom in developing a Set of Relationship Guidelines which the General Assembly would be asked to adopt for the guidance of general agencies accountable to the Assembly. These guidelines are viewed by the committee as reasonable expectations, ones open where ministry needs justify and limiting where limitation clearly appears necessary.

Proposed Relationship Guidelines

Any general agency, commission, division or committee, accountable to the General Assembly of the Church of God in the United States, which chooses to relate in any manner to any working unit associated with the National Council of Churches in Christ or other inter-church body should do so only within the assumptions, affirmations and limitations contained in the following guidelines:

29

1. Any inter-church relationship should be guided by the clear understanding that the Church of God, as represented by the Executive Council and the General Assembly, has not and should not become formal institutional members of the National Council of Churches in Christ. Such organizational identity is not the best way to express Christian unity!
2. Any inter-church body involved in a relationship should be committed publicly to the divinity and lordship of Jesus Christ. He is central to the meaning and the mission of the church!
3. Inter-church relationships should be seen as opportunities to serve and witness in light of the distinctive heritage of the Church of God reformation movement. We have something important to share as well as receive in any such relationship!
4. An inter-church relationship should not be maintained if that relationship gives support to beliefs or actions which clearly violate beliefs or actions generally held to be true and proper by the Church of God reformation movement. We in the Church of God must be accountable to each other and maintain the integrity of our doctrinal heritage!
5. Any Church of God participants in an inter-church relationship should not attempt to speak in the inter-church setting for the Church of God reformation movement as a whole. Participants always should make clear that they function by individual or agency choice and do not necessarily represent their brothers and sisters at large!
6. Church of God general agency staff or dollar resources invested in an inter-church relationship should be limited to the ministry function justifying that relationship. The Church of god does not control and sometimes does not condone all that large inter-church bodies say and do!

Postscript

The study committee wishes to affirm an important call issued to the Church of God by the Consultation on Mission and Ministry of the Church of God in 1984. It was a call "to expand ministries through voluntary relationships with church groups outside the Church of God reformation movement" so that we can "achieve our mission more effectively and expand our ministries." This present committee report and the relationship guidelines proposed above are intended to support, not impede this call. It is the committee's hope that such guidelines will enrich appropriate inter-church relationships and, at the same time, avoid inappropriate ones. It also is our hope that the Church of God will give continuing attention to the opportunities associated with working relationships among Christians for the sake of the church's mission in the world.

B. Identification of *Reformation Principles*

25. General Assembly Reserves a Right

For many years the General Assembly has reserved for itself the right to define its own membership, partly by the potential process of passing judgment on adherence to "general reformation principles." Article III of the 1980 revision of the Constitution of the General Assembly, for example, reads:

The Assembly shall be regarded as a voluntary association. It shall not exercise ecclesiastical jurisdiction or authority over the Church in general nor over individual congregations in particular. But it shall, however, retain the right of a voluntary association to define its own membership and to declare, on occasion, when individual ministers or congregations are not recognized by the Assembly as adhering to the general reformation principles to which the Assembly itself is committed.

Two other related matters are crucial to note. One was a positive assembly action in 1990. It regarded the status of persons whose names were appearing on assembly ballots (nominated by various national bodies) but who were not attending or supporting local congregations of the Church of God. That action follows.

WHEREAS some members of this General Assembly of the Church of God are very much concerned about the appearing in the ballots of names or persons who are not attending or supporting local congregations of the Church of God; and

WHEREAS these persons are being placed into positions of vital importance to this reformation, i.e., college boards of trustees and agencies; and

WHEREAS many of us in this Assembly recognize the latent danger to the biblical and historical message of this reformation movement by such continuing practices; be it

RESOLVED, That all future "Who's Who" for General Assembly balloting include in parentheses the home congregation of said candidates, that we of this Assembly may be better informed and thus enabled to vote more intelligently.

The other related matter involved a negative assembly action. In 1991 the assembly addressed an issue related to religious affiliation and assembly elections or ratifications. In 1990 a motion had been introduced calling for the assembly to "go on record as requesting that all agencies, committees or commissions not place on ballots to be presented to this Assembly for election or ratification the names of persons who do not attend or support local congregations of the Church of God." This motion was referred for study by the Commission on Christian Higher Education. In the assembly of 1991, then, the Commission recommended that the 1990 motion not be adopted. The assembly concurred. The commission's report included an extended rationale, summarized by these concluding paragraphs:

Careful review by the Commission on Christian Higher Education has revealed that adequate criteria are in place for membership on all our boards and that sensitivity to and compatibility with the message and tradition of the Church of God have been considered in nomination processes. The colleges in particulars have missions which, in part, involve their positioning themselves for service in the larger arena of the Christian community and sometimes beyond to the general public. These missions call for creative and courageous flexibility and they need increased attention and understanding both by the church and the other constituencies being served.

An absolute restriction against any inclusion in collegiate governance structures of committed Christians with unusual understanding and influence who may not be actively affiliated with the Church of God would seriously hinder the accomplishment of institutional missions. Thus the Commission recommends that no additional restrictions be placed on the nomination processes of the several boards.

Thus, in summary, there is the assembly expectation that persons to be associated with the assembly will be "in fellowship and doctrinal unity" and it is preferred that typically they will be living out their lives of discipleship in relation to Church of God congregations. Doctrinal unity is to be defined by the direct teaching of the Bible (see entry 27).

26. Executive Council Can Decide Adherence to Reformation Principles

June 1977

WHEREAS Article III of the constitution vests in this General Assembly of the Church of God the authority "to declare on occasion, when individual ministers or congregations are not recognized by the Assembly as adhering to the general reformation principles to which the Assembly itself is committed"; and

WHEREAS this body only meets regularly one time annually; and

WHEREAS this General Assembly has heretofore caused to be created an Executive Council of the Church of God, Inc. with specific purposes, including the following:

Section 3b—"To coordinate the work of the general agencies of the Church of God in their inter-related and cooperative aspects as authorized by the General Assembly"; and

WHEREAS the General Assembly finds it necessary and expedient to delegate to the said Executive Council of the Church of God, Inc. between the annual meetings of the General Assembly, its authority to declare on occasion, when individual ministers or congregations are not recognized as adhering to the general reformation principles and practices to which the Assembly itself is committed; and

WHEREAS this General Assembly finds the above quoted language of Article III of its Constitution to include authority to find that a minister

32

or congregation is no longer in fellowship and doctrinal unity with the Church of God; now, therefore, be it

RESOLVED, That its above quoted authority under Article III of its Constitution be hereby delegated to the Executive Council of the Church of God, Inc. to exercise in its sole discretion between annual meetings of this General Assembly.

Editor's note: Until the 1981 General Assembly none of these "general reformation principles" had been identified formally by the assembly. In 1981, however, one such principle was identified. It was the principle of the central authority of the Bible in the life of the Church. The statement of this principle follows (see entry 27).

27. Biblical Authority in the Life of the Church

June 1981

During 1980-81 concern was expressed across the church that the authority of the Bible in the life of the church needed to be reaffirmed pointedly and publicly. Resolutions seeking to accomplish this purpose were passed in at least two area fellowships of ministers. These resolutions, however, contained "inerrancy" and "binding" language. Such language aroused widespread opposition, including arguments that inerrancy, as popularly understood, is a controversial theory of the Bible's inspiration not clearly taught by the Bible itself and not accepted by millions of evangelical Christians and scholars. Further, the call to "bind" was said to be contrary to the constitution of the General Assembly and alien to the heritage of the reformation movement of the Church of God.

A new resolution finally was drafted by a group of concerned ministers in an attempt to accomplish the central intent of the area fellowships without including the controversial concepts of "inerrancy" and "binding." This resolution eventually was presented to the General Assembly, but with the word requirement added in the final paragraph at the last minute by the Business Committee of the Assembly. The Assembly, however, acted to reinstate the word expectation, thereby maintaining integrity with its understanding of its own constitution and clearly affirming its opposition to the very idea of binding creedal statements being established in the church.

The following, then, is the resolution as finally approved. It is a clear statement of a "reformation principle" to which the Assembly is committed, namely, the genuine inspiration and central authority of the Bible in the life of the church.

PREFACE

For a century the reformation movement of the Church of God has proclaimed a vision of the Church which transcends the artificial and divisive barriers of rigid denominational structure and restrictive creedal statement. In this context, the General Assembly of the Church of God has limited itself as follows:

"This Assembly shall be regarded as a voluntary association. It shall not exercise ecclesiastical jurisdiction or authority over the Church in general nor over individual congregations in particular. But it shall, however, retain the right of a voluntary association to define its own membership and to declare, on occasion, when individual ministers or congregations are not recognized by the Assembly as adhering to the general reformation principles to which the Assembly itself is committed."

The continuing rightness of this self-limitation of the General Assembly is recognized and reaffirmed.

Without intending to exercise ecclesiastical authority, this General Assembly nonetheless desires to record its convictions and expectations in regard to the authority of the Bible in the life of today's church. The following, then, states a general reformation principle to which this Assembly is committed.

RESOLUTION

WHEREAS the intent of this resolution is to be understood in the light of the self-limitation of the General Assembly as stated in its Constitution (as quoted above) and is meant in no way to violate the reformation principle that "the spirit of the movement is to acknowledge good wherever found and to regard no door into the church other than salvation and no test of fellowship other than true Christianity possessed within the heart" (A. L. Byers, *Birth of a Reformation*, Anderson, Indiana: Gospel Trumpet Company, 1921); and

WHEREAS from its beginning the reformation movement of the Church of God has been committed to the general theological stance that the Bible is our only creed and Christ alone is Lord, so that the Bible, supported by the interpretative ministry of the Holy Spirit, has had a central significance among us; and

WHEREAS a public restatement of this historic commitment to the authority of the Bible in the life of the Church appears timely in light of the secular humanism and doctrinal confusions of our day; therefore, be it

RESOLVED, That this Assembly declare its convictions that the Bible truly is the divinely inspired and infallible Word of God. The Bible is without error in all that it affirms, in accordance with its own purpose, namely that it is "profitable for teaching, for reproof, for correction, for training in righteousness, that the man of God may be adequate, equipped for every good work" (2 Timothy 3:16-17, NAS), and it therefore is fully trustworthy and authoritative as the infallible guide for understanding the Christian faith and living the Christian life; and be it further

RESOLVED, That this Assembly call the reformation movement of the Church of God to a new dedication to faithful biblical scholarship and proclamation, based both upon a commitment to its authority as described above and upon a fresh quest for studied insight and divine guidance in

34

the crucial tasks of responsible biblical interpretation, teaching and preaching; and be it further

RESOLVED, That this Assembly state its expectation that all programs within this reformation movement of the Church of God reflect a genuine commitment to the Bible as the inspired and authoritative Word of God; and be it finally

RESOLVED, That this Assembly state its expectation that governing boards and elected officials, charged with oversight of the operational policies of agencies and the credentials of ministers related to this Assembly, will act responsibly and forthrightly in establishing the central significance of the authority of the Bible and in interpreting and implementing the teachings and directives of the Bible in their respective areas of the work of the Church.

Editor's note: As one way of fulfilling this concern, in the 1991 Assembly a resolution was passed endorsing the "Discover Life In Daily Bible Reading" program and urging every congregation to enlist persons in reading through the Bible during 1992.

C. Distribution of Resources

28. Establishment of a Coordinated Budget Plan

June 1927

The 1927 General Ministerial Assembly received favorably the report of the Coordinated Budget Plan Committee. R. L. Berry presented the plan, which previously had been agreed upon by the various national boards. It called for "boards or agencies having work that calls for general church support" to prepare annual budgets which would be examined by a "General Budget Committee." This committee would then "determine the sum to be set as the goal for each individual cause." It further called for "the program coordination of all promotional plans, whether of advertising or of special field representatives" and it designated guidelines for the distribution of designated and undesignated gifts. Finally, the assembly, prepared to activate this plan immediately, authorized its chairman, Charles E. Brown, to appoint five members to this General Budget Committee.

The concept of "Associated Budgets" was implemented in the years to follow. By 1941 the unified effort was known as "The World Service Commission." After reorganization of the Executive Council in 1955, the name was changed to the "Division of World Service."

29. Allocation of World Service Budgets

The following are percentages of the annual World Service budget as approved by the General Assembly of the Church of God for national solicitation and formula distribution to the several agencies and causes listed. The total budget figure used for determining these percentages included all basic, nonleveled, and restricted categories for each year in question except for anticipated relay, budget promotion, and treasury/ stewardship transactions and expenditures.

Allocation of World Service Budgets

MISSIONS	1970-71	1975-76	1980-81	1985-86	1990-91	1991-92
Missionary Board	35.05	38.40	36.47	38.57	39.84	37.72
Mission Latin America	3.41	0.00	0.00	0.00	0.00	0.00
Church Extension/ Home Missions	14.79	13.14	8.63	10.50	10.36	10.21
Hope Hill Children's Home	0.00	0.00	3.22	3.45	3.15	3.23
Mass Communications	4.10	3.07	3.78	3.74	4.26	4.62
Literature Evangelism	0.95	0.77	0.46	0.00	0.00	0.00
Disaster Fund	0.00	0.53	0.08	0.00	0.00	0.00
World Hunger	0.00	1.33	1.54	2.27	2.10	2.04
Million for Missions	0.00	0.00	3.45	0.00	0.00	0.00
TV Special	0.00	0.00	3.84	0.00	0.00	0.00
Church Planting	0.00	0.00	0.00	0.00	0.23	0.00
(SUB TOTAL)	58.30	57.24	61.47	58.53	59.94	57.82
EDUCATION						
School of Theology	0.00	4.77	3.96	4.41	4.16	3.83
Seminary Tuition Fund	0.00	2.12	1.84	1.75	1.52	1.40
Anderson University	11.65	6.02	6.98	7.31	6.72	6.39
GBC/Mid-America Bible College	4.42	4.61	3.85	5.24	7.26	11.07
Mission GBC Completion	0.00	4.37	0.00	0.00	0.00	0.00
Warner Pacific College	7.56	6.47	7.21	7.10	6.03	5.74
Board of Christian Education	5.51	4.99	4.82	5.65	5.46	5.26
Black Ministerial Education	0.00	0.00	1.15	0.00	0.00	0.00
(SUB TOTAL)	29.14	33.35	29.81	31.46	31.15	33.69
SERVICE						
Executive Council/ General Service	3.87	3.84	3.62	7.61	6.98	6.65
Special Committee	0.00	0.00	0.00	0.00	0.06	0.05
Properties/ General Assembly	4.42	2.86	2.86	0.00	0.00	0.00
Board of Pensions	1.91	1.14	1.05	1.11	0.49	0.53
Division of Church Service	1.68	1.12	0.85	0.99	0.96	0.92
Ministers Aid	0.68	0.45	0.34	0.30	0.42	0.34
(SUB TOTAL)	12.56	9.41	8.72	10.01	8.91	8.49
TOTAL	100.00	100.00	100.00	100.00	100.00	100.00

30. Giving Response of the Church

The following total given figures include all giving that received credit from the Division of World Service, including any relay funds handled.

YEAR	MEMBERS	PER CAPITA	INCREASE (DECREASE)	TOTAL GIVING	INCREASE (DECREASE)
1970	147,752	16.36	8.4%	$2,416,513	9.1%
1971	150,198	17.20	5.1%	$2,582,497	6.9%
1972	152,787	17.04	-0.9%	$2,603,428	0.8%
1973	158,264	18.51	8.6%	$2.930,226	12.6%
1974	159,733	20.05	8.3%	$3,202,307	9.3%
1975	165,928	22.96	14.5%	$3,809,844	19.0%
1976	169,372	26.12	13.8%	$4,423,982	16.1%
1977	172,756	27.57	5.6%	$4,762,919	7.7%
1978	173,940	30.98	12.4%	$5,388,512	13.1%
1979	175,405	34.93	12.8%	$6,126,234	13.7%
1980	177,407	37.20	6.5%	$6,599,349	7.7%
1981	180,772	38.99	4.8%	$7,047,486	6.8%
1982	187,485	38.69	-0.8%	$7,254,160	2.9%
1983	191,508	38.82	0.3%	$7,433,992	2.5%
1984	195,105	38.14	-1.8%	$7,440,912	0.1%
1985	197,713	40.04	5.0%	$7,916,592	6.4%
1986	197,625	41.82	4.4%	$8,264,513	4.4%
1987	198,535	41.25	-1.4%	$8,189,467	-0.9%
1988	203,552	40.90	-0.8%	$8,325,940	1.7%
1989	200,062	42.65	4.3%	$8,533,130	2.5%
1990	202,215	42.54	-0.3%	$8,601,648	0.8%
1991	206,445	42.60	0.1%	$8,745,147	1.7%

D. Christian Higher Education

31. Proper Restrictions for a Church College

June 1918

The establishment of Anderson Bible Training School in 1917 was seen by many in the church as a questionable or even dangerous event. In the 1918 General Ministerial Assembly the following report from a specially appointed committee was read and accepted.

Your committee appointed for the purpose of considering restrictions for the Anderson Bible Training School submits the following report:

1. We believe that such a school can be conducted to the glory of God and the welfare of the ministry and church if kept within certain bounds.
2. We believe that no effort should be made to create a sentiment to the effect that young ministers must attend this school in order to secure recognition.

3. It is our opinion that in many cases the education of ministers can best be obtained in those sections of the country where their ministerial work is to be done so that the practical can be more definitely combined with the theoretical. In other words, we do not believe that the Anderson Bible School should supersede or replace other training schools of the church.

4. Students should be left free to choose their own course of study from among such branches as the school provides.

5. No recommendation or diploma should be given any student. Satisfactory gradings in school constitutes no proof that an individual is called of God to preach the gospel. Hence every student must be left on his own responsibility so that he will not possess in this respect any authority proceeding from this school which will give him an advantage over those ministers who have not attended school. In the Church of God every minister must stand on his own merits and earn his place of responsibility whether educated or uneducated.

6. We believe that the training of ministers in this school should include more than their intellectual development along educational lines. The most prominent feature must be their personal development in spirituality, faith, and the gifts of the Spirit of God.

32. Anderson Bible Training School Separated from the Gospel Trumpet Company

June 1925

WHEREAS the Anderson Bible Training School has heretofore been a part of the Gospel Trumpet Company's sphere of responsibility, but has outgrown the meager organization provided for it in the company's ByLaws; and

WHEREAS it represents one of the general phases of the work of the church and requires that it be constituted a legal entity; and

WHEREAS it desires to be separated from the Gospel Trumpet Company and organized in accordance with the same general principles upon which the other general boards of the church are organized; and

WHEREAS the Gospel Trumpet Company has thoroughly considered and approved the separation, as well as the school's proposed Articles of Association as now modified; therefore, be it

RESOLVED, That this Assembly approves the proposal to have the school separated from said company, and organized in the manner desired.

33. Pacific Bible College Becomes a National Agency

June 1956

The 1956 General Ministerial Assembly voted the necessary changes in its own bylaws to establish Pacific Bible College as a subordinate board of the assembly. In 1959 the assembly concurred with the action of the college's board of trustees changing the school's name to Warner Pacific College. In 1970 the assembly took major action in assisting the college in a time of financial crisis.

34. Establishment of the Commission on Christian Higher Education

June 1958

WHEREAS the study Commission on Higher Education, authorized by this General Ministerial Assembly in June 1952, after five years of study and research, is convinced of the need of a permanent Commission on Higher Education, a conviction shared by those connected with our educational institutions as well as by ministers and laymen; be it therefore

RESOLVED, That this General Ministerial Assembly hereby authorizes the creation of a permanent Commission on Higher Education as outlined in the By-Laws herewith submitted, whose general purpose shall be to promote the cause of Christian higher education within the Church of God Movement, said commission to function within the framework of the Executive Council, and be it further

RESOLVED, That immediately upon adoption of this resolution and its accompanying By-Laws, the educational institutions named in these By-Laws, the Board of Christian Education and the Executive Council be hereby instructed to appoint those persons who shall constitute the commission.

35. Policy on Starting New Colleges

June 1964

In this time of growth in higher education in America many church colleges are finding it increasingly difficult to remain in operation or to uncover the resources necessary for an adequate program. Within the Church of God it appears evident that (1) at present there are enough colleges to serve the Church of God student population able and willing to attend those colleges; (2) adequate support is not being provided for existing colleges, most of which are struggling financially for their very lives; and (3) new colleges in the Church continually enter the talking-planning stage, are presumably designed to meet the needs of a particular geographic area, but generally are without adequate student and financial support necessary for existence and growth.

The Commission on Christian Higher Education of the Church of God believes it is imperative that great caution be exercised in the establishment of new Church of God colleges, acknowledging that considerable hurt may derive to the Church and its young people through a college not built on an adequate foundation. Specifically,

—We urge that a new college be contemplated only within the

framework of careful consultation with the Commission on Christian Higher Education, recognizing that through this means we are most likely to achieve the coordination so necessary to the total advancement of higher education in the Church;

—We urge that in the establishment of any new college, careful plans be developed for financial support and underwriting recognizing that the costs of maintaining an adequate program at the college level are enormous;

—We insist that if a prospective college would ever expect or hope to seek the support and assistance of the total Church, it should seek that support and assistance in the crucial stages of planning and establishment.

The Commission on Christian Higher Education continues to make itself available to the Church and its educational institutions as a resource, a stimulus, and a guide in these days of unusual problems and opportunities in the Church and in higher education.

36. Gulf-Coast Becomes a National Agency

June 1968

WHEREAS Gulf-Coast Bible College, Houston, Texas, has served the Church of God since September 1953 as an institution of higher education and during these years has trained an increasing number of young people for Christian service; and

WHEREAS the Texas State Assembly of the Church of God, to which Gulf-Coast Bible College is responsible organizationally, adopted a resolution in 1963 with the knowledge of, and concurrence in, by the trustees of Gulf-Coast Bible College that requested the Executive Council of the Church of God that the college be permitted to share in the budget for higher education through World Service; and

WHEREAS at that time, in the judgment of the Executive Council, Gulf-Coast Bible College had not attained the status of a general agency of the Church of God and therefore the request was referred to the Commission on Christian Higher Education for study in depth and to recommend guidelines to the college in obtaining additional strength and to make recommendations to the Executive Council for further consideration of the request from the Texas State Assembly; and

WHEREAS during the past five years Gulf-Coast Bible College has cooperated closely with the Commission on Christian Higher Education in making a self-study and in the implementation of recommended guidelines whereby the college might obtain accreditation by the American Association of Bible Colleges (Gulf-Coast Bible College now holds an associate membership in the American Association of Bible Colleges and is working toward possible full accreditation in 1968); and

WHEREAS the Board of Trustees of Gulf-Coast Bible College and the members of the Texas State Assembly of the Church of God, in keeping with their indicated desire for the college to have the status of a general agency of the Church of God, have approved provisional changes in the charter, articles of association, and bylaws of the college in order to comply with the requirements of the bylaws of the General Assembly of the Church of God as pertains to a general agency and, by so doing, have indicated their willingness to abide by the regulations, privileges, and limitations of a general agency, and as a member within the family of agencies, organized by and responsible to the General Assembly of the Church of God; and

WHEREAS the Executive Council of the Church of God, in session February 21, 1968, voted (23-3) to recommend to the General Assembly of the Church of God that recognition be given to Gulf-Coast Bible College as a general agency of the Church of God; therefore be it

RESOLVED, That the members of the General Assembly of the Church of God, in session on June 18, 1968, recognize Gulf-Coast Bible College as a general agency of the Church of God, with understanding that such recognition will entitle Gulf-Coast Bible College to have representation in the membership of the Executive Council, and participation in the World Service Budget; and be it further

RESOLVED, That the Executive Council be authorized by the General Assembly to work with the Texas State Assembly and the Board of Trustees of Gulf-Coast Bible College in the implementation of this action.

37. Action Concerning the "Foundation for Religious Studies"

June 1972

During 1971-1972, in the face of low enrollments, rising costs, and an apparent need for revitalizing the curriculum, the board of trustees set in motion a series of changes in the School of Theology. Included was the establishment of the Center for Pastoral Studies and an affiliation with the Foundation for Religious Studies (a consortium of theological schools in Indianapolis, Indiana). The following resolution was offered:

WHEREAS we, members of the Board of Trustees of Anderson College, are assured that the effective education of pastors, evangelists, missionaries, and other Christian teachers and workers, is one of the most urgent needs of the Church; and

WHEREAS this Board of Trustees, in its search to determine what set of relationships and circumstances will provide the best training and preparation for the ministry in the Church of God, initiated a major study of theological education during the past year through the appointment of a special committee composed of the chairman of the General Assembly, the executive secretary of the Executive Council, College and School of Theology administrators, and members appointed from the Board of Trustees; and

WHEREAS the committee, through its year-long study took testimony from pastors, faculty members, School of Theology alumni, and present students; and

41

WHEREAS the recommendations of the committee included the development of new and expanded programs in the School of Theology, including a Center for Pastoral Studies and certain cooperative relationships with the Foundation for Religious Studies and Asbury Theological Seminary; and

WHEREAS the expanded programming makes available new resources for theological education in the Church of God and lays greater emphasis on preaching, evangelism, and field work experiences; and

WHEREAS this board feels that the expanded program will result in well-prepared ministers who are able to preach the Word effectively, teach, counsel, evangelize, and build up the Church; and

WHEREAS certain questions have been raised relating to the scope and involvements of the expanded School of Theology program, be it, therefore,

RESOLVED, That the General Assembly of the Church of God, meeting in annual session in Anderson, Indiana, on the 20th day of June, 1972, call for the establishment of a special committee, composed of three (3) pastors appointed by the chairman of the General Assembly, two (2) members of the Anderson College Board of Trustees, and two (2) members appointed by the Commission on Christian Higher Education of the Church of God, to make a study of the School of Theology expanded program during its third year, to assess the effectiveness of the program for the preparation of ministers for the Church of God, and to present a report to the Board of Trustees and the General Assembly.

Editor's note: The above resolution was defeated. It was replaced by the following resolution, which was adopted by a 499-422 ballot vote.

In view of the defeat of the resolution establishing a social committee to study theological education, we the following ministers whose names appear below,

Hereby move that the association with the Foundation for Religious Studies be dissolved within the next three months or at the end of the first semester of the academic year.

38. Recommendations of the Study Committee on the Seminary

June 1973

The 1972 General Assembly authorized a one-year study committee to bring to the 1973 assembly a report containing "recommendations for the continuation of a Church of God seminary, responsible to the General Assembly." A major report was so brought. It included a series of observations and suggestions and twelve specific recommendations. The total report was received and approved by the assembly. The following is a brief summary of the recommendations with page references to the fuller statement of each within the report itself.

42

1. Commission on Christian Higher Education consider broadening program of Center for Pastoral Studies (page 7).
2. World Service Budget show askings of both graduate School of Theology and Anderson College undergraduate program (page 8).
3. Move toward increased World Service support to School of Theology (page 8).
4. Move toward per-student base in Anderson College support (page 8).
5. Budget Committee bring viable plan to achieve goals for Assembly review in June 1974 (page 8).
6. Promote for scholarship funds (page 8).
7. Executive Council establish Special Trust Fund (page 9).
8. Commission on Christian Higher Education give high priority to seminary needs and problems (page 9).
9. Provide for additional meetings of Commission on Christian Higher Education (page 9).
10. Establish "blue ribbon" committee to give particular and continuing attention to School of Theology (page 9).
11. Assembly ratification of dean (page 9).
12. In June 1977, General Assembly again test thesis of free-standing seminary (page 10).

39. Seminary Budget in World Service

June 1974

The chair again recognized F. Eugene Fauntleroy, who called attention to a report titled "Budget Committee Recommendations" regarding a recommended increase of $40,000 in the basic budget allocation to Anderson College for its School of Theology in the 1974-75 World Service Budget and that the Division of World Service concur with the Budget Committee in recommending to the 1974 General Assembly that this plan of additional support to Anderson College be extended over the following four years, or through the 1978-79 World Service year. A copy of these recommendations and the assumptions upon which the Budget Committee based them is attached to the original minutes.

Eugene Fauntleroy moved the adoption of these recommendations, seconded by Dan Harman. Eugene Fauntleroy clarified the five-year proposal as amounting to $200,000 by 1978-79. Motion carried.

40. Seminary Tuition Aid Fund

June 1974

The chair recognized G. David Cox, chairman of the Seminary Advisory Committee.

G. David Cox moved the adoption of a resolution from the Seminary Advisory Committee, to wit, "that the General Assembly instruct the

Division of World Service to establish strategy for raising a goal of $50,000 for the year 1974-75 to be retained as a separate account established by the School of Theology, to be activated in the 1975-76 year, for the purpose of defraying tuitional costs now required from the students. These funds are to be expended for tuition costs for Church of God students in the School of Theology and, if available, also for extraordinary moving expenses and then also for student aid in exceptional situations. This dollar goal should be reviewed annually by the Budget Committee and made a part of the World Service Budget." This resolution was approved by the General Assembly.

41. Relationship of Seminary to Anderson College

June 1976

WHEREAS the General Assembly of the Church of God, in its June 21, 1971 meeting, charged the Commission on Christian Higher Education to make a thorough and extensive study of theological education and ministerial training in the Church of God; and

WHEREAS the General Assembly, on June 19, 1972, approved the appointment of a Special Advisory Committee to advise with the board of trustees and administrative staff of Anderson College regarding the program of the School of Theology, with the stipulation that this committee was to function "until the completion of the study which the Assembly in its June 1972 session requested the Commission on Christian Higher Education to make, but not beyond June 1977"; and

WHEREAS the Commission on Christian Higher Education has now completed its study and submitted its report to the General Assembly; and

WHEREAS the Seminary Advisory Committee, in a communication under date of March 15, 1976, has communicated the following information to the Commission on Christian Higher Education, to wit:

"We, the Seminary Advisory Committee of the General Assembly, unanimously and strongly reaffirm and wish to further encourage the concept set forth by the General Assembly's Special Study Committee in its major report to the Assembly in 1973 that there must be 'a willingness and commitment in the Church of God to concentrate its graduate and ministerial education in the seminary.'

"In the light of our work over the past three years and in the light of the very encouraging developments in the School of Theology during that period, we, the Seminary Advisory Committee of the General Assembly, see no reason to consider further the question of a free-standing seminary, and we hereby encourage the Commission on Christian Higher Education to concur in this judgment and to so recommend to the General Assembly in its 1976 report." And

WHEREAS the Commission on Christian Higher Education, in its meeting on May 1, 1976, did consider the recommendation from the Seminary Advisory Committee, and did wholeheartedly concur in it; therefore, be it

RESOLVED, That the General Assembly of the Church of God affirm this recommendation mutually agreed upon by the Seminary Advisory Committee and the Commission on Christian Higher Education; and grant its approval, for the present time, for the seminary—the graduate School of Theology—to remain in coordinate relationship to, and under the administrative guidance of, the Anderson College Board of Trustees and its administrative officers; and be it further

RESOLVED, That special commendation be given to the board of trustees and administrative officers of Anderson College for the attention they have given to the School of Theology over the past four years; to the Seminary Advisory Committee for the excellent work they have done in keeping the needs of the School of Theology before the General Assembly; and to the pastors and congregations that have shown concern in the seminary by becoming convenant churches in the seminary internship program and in helping to underwrite the tuition costs of eligible ministerial students; and be it further

RESOLVED, That the General Assembly, by its adoption of this resolution, consider the work of the Seminary Advisory Committee terminated and that the assignment of the Commission on Christian Higher Education in regard to theological education and ministerial training is now complete.

42. Recommendations for Ministerial Education

June 1976

The 1972 General Assembly was the scene of extended debate over matters related to the training of ministers (see entry 37). One result of that debate was a charge to the Commission on Christian Higher Education "to make a thorough and extensive study of theological and ministerial training in the Church of God."

The 1976 General Assembly received and approved the final result of this commission study which was presented in the form of a lengthy written report. Included was a set of affirmations and proposals. These are to be found on pages 536-541 of *The First Century*, volume II, by Barry L. Callen (Anderson, Indiana: Warner Press, 1979).

43. Black Ministerial Education Fund

June 1977

As part of its study the Commission on Christian Higher Education reviewed the statement in the Bylaws of the General Assembly pertaining to general agencies and the document adopted by the Executive Council in 1965 titled What Is a General Agency. In the light of the provisions in the Bylaws of the Assembly and the findings of its study, the commission and consultants unanimously agreed not to recommend general agency status for Bay Ridge Christian College. It was agreed that an alternative to general agency status would be in the best interest of training black leaders to serve the Church of God at the present time.

The following resolution was presented and approved to accomplish this purpose:

WHEREAS in June 1975, the General Assembly of the Church of God referred a request from the Southern Association of the Church of God to the Commission on Christian Higher Education concerning potential general agency status for Bay Ridge Christian College; and

WHEREAS the General Assembly recommended to the commission a thorough study of the best way to train leaders to serve the black church in the South, to include an in-depth study of Bay Ridge Christian College if needed; and assistance of a team of black consultants and with the full cooperation of the administration of Bay Ridge Christian College and representatives of the Southern Association of the Church of God; and

WHEREAS the Commission on Christian Higher Education and its eight black consultants have unanimously agreed as a result of these studies that the need is urgent, complex in nature, and national in scope, necessitating an approach other than the recommendation of General Agency status for Bay Ridge Christian College; therefore, be it

RESOLVED, That the General Assembly of the Church of God establish within the annual budget of the Commission on Christian Higher Education, beginning with the 1977-78 budget, a Fund for Black Ministerial Education; and be it further

RESOLVED, That the administration of the fund be done in consultation with representative black leaders of the Church of God; and be it further

RESOLVED, That the commission in the administration of this fund give priority consideration to the following areas of need: (a) the urgent need for the development of the academic program of Bay Ridge Christian College, (b) the underwriting of scholarships for eligible black ministerial students to attend Church of God colleges, and (c) the development, in cooperation with the Center for Pastoral Studies, of an in-service training program designed primarily for black church leaders with limited formal training; and be it further

RESOLVED, That in the World Service Budget for 1977-78, the Fund for Black Ministerial Education be $55,000, with the understanding that gifts for this purpose would receive World Service credit; and be it further

RESOLVED, That the Boards of Trustees of Bay Ridge Christian College and Gulf-Coast Bible College be encouraged to explore the possibilities of joint programming and other mutual uses of the available human and material resources and that each of these institutions give annual progress reports in this regard to the Commission on Christian Higher Education; and be it finally

RESOLVED, That the commission be instructed to make an intensive evaluation of the fund and the above programming during 1979-80 and that the commission make a report to the General Assembly.

Editor's note: Based on the research and recommendation of the Commission on Christian Higher Education, the 1981 General Assembly acted to discontinue this fund. This action included the future granting of World Service credit for funds channeled through World Service for Bay Ridge Christian College and a continuing assignment for the commission to identify and address "the gaps or stortcomings" of the several national programs of black ministerial education.

44. Anderson College Board Speaks to the Church

June 1981

On 16 June 1981 the Board of Trustees of Anderson College made a major report to the General Assembly. This report spoke directly to concerns of the assembly as these had been focused by a select committee that worked with high national visibility between the 1980 and 1981 assemblies. The concerns centered on certain of the existing policies and personnel of the college, including questions of clarification regarding the nature of the school's mission, particularly as that mission related to the church and its stated convictions.

Following lengthy discussion, the assembly voted overwhelmingly that:

The General Assembly register its appreciation for the thorough manner in which the Board of Trustees of Anderson College addressed the recommendations of the Select Committee, and that the General Assembly accept the report and commit itself to work with the college in the realization of these objectives.

45. Church and Colleges: A Call for Clarification

June 1981

The 1981 General Assembly accepted with appreciation a major report from the Board of Trustees of Anderson College. In a section of that report identified as "Critical issues ahead," there was a call for clarification of the relationship between the church and its colleges.

It read:

"Historically, the relationship of the Church of God to its colleges has been largely informal and undefined. There has been the relationship created by the election of trustees, the ratification of chief executive officers, budgetary support and general reporting. However, there is little clarity regarding the Church's expectations of its colleges and there has not been a widespread understanding of what constitutes a responsible relationship between a church body and its institutions of higher learning. We urge an exploration of this subject."

46. Gardner Bible College—50th Anniversary

June 1983

WHEREAS Gardner Bible College, this year of 1983-84, will be celebrating its 50th year of service to the Church of God, and

WHEREAS Gardner Bible College is the second oldest institution of higher education in North America of the Church of God, and

WHEREAS the Gardner Board, its faculty and staff, and the General Assemblies of both Western Canada and Ontario, have reviewed the original purpose of the school and have affirmed its viability for the present and future and have recommitted themselves to that purpose (original purpose stated below), and

WHEREAS Gardner Bible College is filling a significant role in the brotherhood of Church of God institutions of higher education, be it, therefore

RESOLVED, That this assembly commend Gardner Bible College on this milestone in its life and ministry, and be it further

RESOLVED, That this assembly call upon the church to enter into celebration with the Canadian church wherever and whenever possible in this year they have set aside as Gardner Bible College's Year of Jubilee.

Respectfully submitted,
Business Committee of this Assembly

Original Purpose as Stated in
THE ACT OF INCORPORATION
By The Province of Alberta
March 31, 1947

THE PURPOSE of Gardner Bible College is the providing of intellectual and spiritual training for prospective ministers, missionaries, and gospel workers and of promoting the true principles and teachings of the Bible as taught and exemplified by Jesus Christ.

47. Support for Move of Gulf-Coast to Oklahoma

June 1984

President Conley of Gulf-Coast Bible College reported to the 1984 General Assembly on the finalized plans of the college to move its operations to Oklahoma City, Oklahoma, in the summer of 1985. Concern was raised from the assembly floor that the assembly should approve such moving plans since such a move would require a change in the college's articles of incorporation and such a change requires assembly approval. A motion emerged from the assembly floor calling for the assembly to approve the moving plan already underway. This motion carried unanimously.

48

48. New Name for Gulf-Coast Bible College

June 1985

The 1985 General Assembly approved the third restated articles of incorporation of Gulf-Coast Bible College. This restatement assumed the school's relocation to Oklahoma City, Oklahoma, and its intent to do business in Oklahoma under the name "Mid-America Bible College."

49. New Process for Electing Warner Pacific Trustees

June 1985

The Board of Trustees of Warner Pacific College recommended and the General Assembly approved the following:
1. That nominations for lay members be voted on at the West Coast Ministerial Assembly with the name of the final candidate brought to the General Assembly for ratification.
2. That the college continue to take nominations for each ministerial position on the Board of Trustees to the West Coast Ministerial Assembly and place the names of two candidates on the ballot of the General Assembly.

Editor's note: A major reason that prompted this change was the lack of acquaintance that many Assembly members had with nominees, particularly laypersons located in the northwest.

50. Reconstituting the Membership of the Commission on Christian Higher Education

June 1985

Following a meeting of the presidents, deans, and board chairs of the Church of God colleges in the United States in November 1984 and the annual meeting of the Commission on Christian Higher Education in January 1985, the following proposal was presented to the Executive Council and then to the General Assembly. It received approval from both bodies. A central assumption was that the proposed new composition of the commission would enhance the commission's functioning by assuring that key decision makers in higher education participate fully in the work of the commission. This action increased the size of the commission and eliminated the category of associate nonvoting members.

Effective 1 July 1985 the commission's membership was established as:
Anderson College president, dean, and board chair   3
Warner Pacific College president, dean, and board chair   3
Mid-America Bible College president, dean, and board chair 3
Bay Ridge Christian College president,
        dean, and board chair   3

Warner Southern College president, dean, and board chair	3
Anderson School of Theology dean	1
Azusa Pacific University president	1
Executive Council representative (staff director)	1
Elected representatives (General Assembly)	6
Board of Christian Education executive secretary	1
Gardner Bible College president, dean, and board chair	3
Total	28

51. Fiftieth Anniversary of Warner Pacific College

June 1986

WHEREAS Warner Pacific College will be celebrating in 1986-87 its fiftieth (50th) year of service to the people and mission of the Church of God, having been founded as Pacific Bible College in Spokane, Washington in 1937; and

WHEREAS the college moved to Portland, Oregon in 1940, changed its name to Warner Pacific College in 1959 and received full accreditation in 1961; and

WHEREAS the college has shared the time of many of its distinguished leaders with the general work of the Church, including Albert F. Gray who served as Chair of this Assembly for fifteen years and Milo L. Chapman who was a long-term member and officer of the Commission on Christian Higher Education; and

WHEREAS these fifty years of the college's existence and service have been characterized by sacrifice and dedication in the quest for excellence, informed by the central convictions of both the Christian faith and higher learning; therefore, be it

RESOLVED, That the General Assembly of the Church of God, in session June 17-18, 1986, join with the Commission on Christian Higher Education in recognizing, commending and thanking Warner Pacific College on this fiftieth anniversary occasion; and be it further

RESOLVED, That this General Assembly of the Church of God call upon the church to enter into the various events of the anniversary celebration and, by so doing, dedicate herself anew to the importance of Christian higher education in these troubled times.

52. Limitation of Terms Exemption

June 1986

In June 1985 the General Assembly placed a limitation of terms on any person serving on the governing board of a national agency. The following year the Commission on Christian Higher Education initiated a request that this limitation be less restrictive for the board memberships of the colleges. The Commission argued that "the functions and procedures of members of the college boards are distinctive. . . ." The assembly agreed, extending to a maximum of fifteen consecutive years the allowable tenure of service of any one person (although after a lapse of one year that person could be renominated). In 1990 this broadened limitation of terms was extended to all persons affected by the original 1985 action. See entry 23.

53. New Name for Anderson College

June 1987

RESOLVED, That this General Assembly of the Church of God, in its annual meeting assembled at Anderson, Indiana, this 17th day of June, 1987, hereby approves the recommendation of the Board of Trustees of Anderson College, Inc., that Article I of the restated Articles of Incorporation of said Anderson College, Inc., be amended, and does hereby adopt the following proposed amended Article I:

"NAME
The name of this Corporation is Anderson University, Inc."

54. The Year of Christian Higher Education

June 1988

WHEREAS the Church of God (Anderson, Indiana) has a long and rich heritage of Christian Higher Education; and

WHEREAS the church supports the following predominantly Church of God colleges and university (Anderson University, Anderson University School of Theology, Bay Ridge Christian College, Gardner Bible College, Mid-America Bible College, Warner Pacific College, and Warner Southern College); and

WHEREAS the Commission on Christian Higher Education is celebrating thirty years of service to the Church of God; and

WHEREAS well equipped lay and clergy leadership will enhance greatly the church's concern for revival, be it

RESOLVED, That this assembly go on record as affirming the ministry of Christian Higher Education; and be it

RESOLVED, That July 1, 1988 to June 30, 1989 be declared jointly as a year of Christian Higher Education and revival; and be it further

RESOLVED, That local congregations, state and regional agencies, and national agencies find ways to promote Christian Higher Education, to sensitize the church to the values of Christian Higher Education, and to lift up the importance of attending a Church of God college/university.

55. Support for Prohibition

June 1928

The prohibition of the sale and use of alcoholic beverages was written into the United States Constitution as the Eighteenth Amendment, effective 1920, but by 1928 Prohibition was being challenged vigorously by some prominent politicians, including attempts to repeal the amendment. The 1928 General Ministerial Assembly spoke clearly.

WHEREAS we regard this propaganda as a challenge to the morality and public welfare, therefore be it

RESOLVED, That we urge a strict enforcement of the present prohibition laws, and be it further

RESOLVED, That we put ourselves upon record as favoring no candidate or political party that favors modification of the present prohibition law.

56. Objection to Peacetime Conscription of Youth

June 1928, 1932, 1947

The General Ministerial Assembly of 1928 spoke sharply against "war as a method of settling international disputes" and declared itself "in favor of every effort being put forward . . . to propagate the principles of peace." Again in 1932 the assembly addressed this subject by stating bluntly that "war is unchristian, futile and suicidal. . . . We will never again sanction or participate in any war." By 1947, with the tragedy of World War II still fresh on all minds, the assembly spoke once again.

WHEREAS this suffering and battered world even yet staggers under the shock of wars past, present, and future; and

WHEREAS the only bright rays of hope appear in the valiant efforts of relief of hunger and suffering abroad and in the aid given toward achieving material and spiritual reconstruction; and

WHEREAS we as a religious body have participated in such efforts and expect to continue to do so to the extent of our abilities; but

WHEREAS there is a vigorous campaign for conscripting the youth of our churches and nation for compulsory peacetime military training; and

WHEREAS the alleged benefits of such training are nullified by exposure to immoral influences coincident with the military life; and

WHEREAS the use of atomic warfare techniques would nullify the use of traditional armed forces; and

WHEREAS such preparation for war is no guarantee of peace, but, rather, creates an atmosphere which crystallizes the threat of war into the actuality; and

WHEREAS education for peacetime pursuits for uplifting mankind would be replaced by education for death and destruction; and

WHEREAS the need of our day is the erasure of malice, suspicion, and misunderstanding; and for the promotion of brotherhood, mutual trust, and the ministry of healing; and

WHEREAS the democratic processes of our government would be threatened by further growth of the military establishment; therefore, be it

RESOLVED, That the General Ministerial Assembly of the Church of God, assembled at Anderson, Indiana, June 18, 1947, commend the leaders of our nation for the splendid work of relief and rehabilitation which they have directed; but be it further

RESOLVED, That we register vigorous objection to any plan for peacetime conscription of youth for military training; and be it further

RESOLVED, That the secretary of this Assembly be instructed to send a copy of this resolution to the President of the United States, to the presiding officers of both houses of Congress, and to their respective military affairs committees, and to the Secretary of War.

57. Supreme Court on Segregation

June 1954

WHEREAS the United States Supreme Court has rendered a decision to end race segregation in the public schools, and

WHEREAS this decision brings to focus certain tensions in the areas of employment, housing, transportation, dining, and other public facilities, and

WHEREAS the principles of brotherhood and unity of God's children without regard to distinctive racial groups have been commonly taught in our movement, therefore, be it

RESOLVED, That this Assembly go on record as being in accord with the spirit and intent of the Supreme Court ruling, and be it further

RESOLVED, That this Assembly recommend to our people:

(1) Restraint, patience, and humility in meeting this problem of segregation;

(2) That they take an active part in study and efforts in their respective communities to find wise means of solving the problems of segregation; and be it further

RESOLVED, That there be a continuous demonstration of Christian brotherhood and unity on these campgrounds, and that there be fair and equitable treatment of all peoples regardless of race or economic status, and

WE FURTHER RECOMMEND that we enter into a covenant of prayer and personal rededication to the end that the will of God be accomplished in the relationships of all people.

58. Federal Tax Funds for Education

June 1961

WHEREAS there has been wide discussion in the public press and in the current session of the Congress of the United States concerning the issue of granting federal funds to education, and

WHEREAS there are many facets of this issue which are of particular concern to the churches of America, therefore, be it

RESOLVED, That we, the General Ministerial Assembly of the Church of God, met in annual session in Anderson, Indiana, this 22nd day of June, 1961, do hereby express the following convictions regarding the use of federal tax funds for education:

1. We reaffirm our confidence in and our support of the public school system as an indispensable means of providing educational opportunity for all children; we recognize the great problems now being faced by the public schools and urge provision for increased resources for the operation and improvement of these public schools within a framework of proper safeguards.
2. We oppose any grants from federal, state, or local tax funds for the operation and support of non-public elementary and secondary schools.
3. We are concerned that the historic principle of separation of church and state be maintained and promoted and urge all branches of the government to avoid any infringement of the ideal of religious liberty which would inevitably arise when taxes paid under compulsion by all people are used to aid non-public schools.

Be it further

RESOLVED, That a copy of this resolution be sent to the President of the United States, and that additional copies be made available to the public press and such other media of communication as may desire them.

59. Separation of Church and State

June 1962

In view of the tremendous pressure now being brought to bear on our federal government for subsidies and handouts by the Roman Catholic church for its parochial school system, it is now apparent that a definite stand needs to be taken by those of us who favor and believe fervently in the separation of church and state. We believe in the basic principle of the sacred nature of man's relationship to God. We do not believe that this can be legislated nor that it should become a part of political jurisdiction which is a direct possibility if we were to accept government aid for parochial systems.

Be it, therefore,

RESOLVED, That a special committee be appointed by the Executive Council of the General Ministerial Assembly to study the field of church-state relationships as it relates to our colleges, agencies, and local church problems and to return to this assembly with a report as to our stand regarding the above-mentioned relationships.

Editor's note: A major report of this special committee dated 17 June 1964 was made available to the assembly and was included with its 1965 minutes. A portion of that report reads as follows:

1. We believe in the public school system as an indispensable means of providing educational opportunity for all children. . . .
2. While supporting the right of religious groups to establish and maintain schools that meet prescribed educational standards at their own expense, and the right of parents to decide whether their children should attend public or non-public schools, we have serious questions concerning:
   a. Grants being made from federal, state, or local tax funds for parochial elementary and secondary schools;
   b. Payments being made from public funds for tuition or scholarships for children to attend private or church-related elementary or secondary schools, and grants being made to parents for that purpose;
   c. Tax credits, tax forgiveness, and exemption from school taxes for parents whose children attend non-public elementary or secondary schools.
3. There seems to be community value in supplying dental or medical and welfare services . . . to all children in any school . . . when assurance is given that such services are known to recipients as public services and expenditures are administered by public authorities who are responsible to the electorate.
4. In any provision of federal funds for tax-supported elementary and secondary public schools:
   a. There be no discrimination among children on the basis of race, religion, class, or national origin;
   b. There be adequate safeguards against federal control of educational policy.

60. Major Statement on Race

June 1964

In order clearly to define our stand as members of the General Ministerial Assembly of the Church of God, and to encourage Christian action, we affirm that:

We base our stand toward basic human rights on the teaching of the Scriptures. God has "made of one blood all nations of men" (Acts 17:26). "For we are all the children of God by faith in Jesus Christ . . . for we are all one in Jesus Christ" (Gal. 3:26, 28). The first of these speaks as to origin, the second as to relationship. We believe that in the Church of God there should be no racial barriers because we are all brethren in Christ. We believe that man was made in the image of God, that every person is of intrinsic worth before God, and that every individual has a right to the fullest possible opportunities for the development of life abundant and eternal. We believe that these rights are given by God and that the church has a responsibility to defend them and work for their guarantee.

Firmly believing that the New Testament teaching sets forth a brotherhood without racial discrimination, we will work to achieve an experience of fairness and honest love toward all our brethren, free from discrimination based on race. This calls for patience, understanding, forgiveness and unselfish service from every member regardless of race. The law of love should be the rule by which we live under all circumstances.

The General Ministerial Assembly defines its membership in this manner:

"Ordained ministers of the Church of God in good and regular standing who are present at any authorized and duly called meeting of the Assembly. Unordained ministers who are pastors or full-time associate pastors of recognized congregations. Laymen who are elected or appointed members of the Executive Council, a subordinate board, committee, or commission of the Assembly."

All members of all races who qualify are urged to participate fully in the Assembly business and to exercise the common privileges granted to all members. Membership on national boards, committees, the program of the International Convention are open on the basis of qualifications. Brethren of all races are urged to seek and develop those qualities which will make their ministries beneficial to the whole church and to remember that the ministry of prayer to undergird those in general responsibilities makes one a partner and co-worker in carrying them out, even though he may not hold an office or be on the program.

We urge ministers of State Assemblies to:

1. Make special efforts to get ministers of all races to work toward a united expression of brotherhood and oneness.
2. Attempt to see that persons, regardless of race, are nominated for committees and offices in the state work according to qualifications.
3. Where there are segregated assemblies, begin the steps which will eventually bring all the brethren into one working fellowship.

We commend the hundreds of our congregations whose life and doors are open to people of all races and urge that they make this fact known by appropriate announcement. We urge that local congregations make special efforts to integrate those of other races who come into their midst. Because strangers may be timid and fearful, special care and concern should be exercised for them.

We urge each individual member to examine his life patterns in the light of the nature of the gospel and to fully welcome into congregational life fellow members and all persons without regard to race, color, or nationality.

We urge all our congregations which have not practiced an open door policy to honestly appraise their position in the light of New Testament teaching and the commitment of the Church of God to its teaching.

We recognize the difficult situation of our brethren where the social pattern is fixed and hostile to the brotherhood of all people. In love we extend confidence to them in their difficult situation. We trust that through prayer they can find ways of applying the principles of brotherhood and human rights even though the environment might be unfriendly.

We urge that we will always be guided by sound biblical principles rather than the highly emotional pitch so prevalent in our world. Ours is a call to prayer and study and deliberate Christian action. We are not called to conform to the demands of the world or society. We are called to follow the Lord and obey Him. This call is to every one of us, regardless of race or culture.

We, the members of the General Ministerial Assembly, pledge our prayers, concerns, and moral support to those pastors, congregations and members who are faithful to their Lord.

61. Civil Rights Legislation

June 1964

WHEREAS our nation is currently confronted with a grave social revolution, and

WHEREAS the nation's conscience has become increasingly aware and sensitive regarding racial discrimination and injustice to minority groups in our nation, and

WHEREAS the United States Constitution gives a clear status in law to a fundamental Christian and American principle—namely, the Constitutional guarantee of equal freedom and equal justice to all citizens, and

WHEREAS there is currently before the United States Senate, civil rights legislation designed to protect the Constitutional rights of all citizens of our nation, and

WHEREAS the Church of God Reformation Movement believes that the principle of segregation based on color, race, caste, or ethnic origin is a denial of the Christian faith and ethic, which stems from the basic premise taught by our Lord that all men are the children of God, be it, therefore,

RESOLVED, That the General Ministerial Assembly of the Church of God in session at Anderson, Indiana, go on record as favoring the passage of that type of civil rights legislation which will guarantee justice and equality to all our citizens regardless of race, nationality, or religion.

62. Constitutional Guarantee of Voting Rights

June 1965

WHEREAS the General Assembly of the Church of God in its 1964 meeting adopted a "Statement on Race Relations" which contains this statement: "The right to choose a place of residence, to enter school, to secure employment, to vote or attend church should in no way be limited by a person's race or culture," and

WHEREAS the 1965 General Assembly continues to bear witness to the stand it has taken in the area of race relations, be it, therefore,

RESOLVED, That the General Assembly of the Church of God in session at Anderson, Indiana, supports legislation in support of Amendment XV of the Constitution of the United States which guarantees equal voting rights for all citizens in all fifty states of the Union without any discrimination based upon racial, religious, or economic differences as early as possible. Be it further

RESOLVED, That a copy of this resolution be mailed to the President of the United States and to the appropriate legislative committees.

63. General Agency Initiatives for Equal Rights

June 1965

WHEREAS the time for making ringing declarations against racial discrimination has passed, having moved from saying to doing, be it, therefore,

RESOLVED, That the General Assembly of the Church of God in session at Anderson, Indiana, encourage and support the general agencies of the Church to take the steps and risks they deem wise and necessary to involve the church more deliberately in the struggle for equal rights.

64. Involvement in Racial Justice

June 1965

WHEREAS the General Assembly in its 1964 June meeting affirmed that we should boldly stand on the principles of basic human rights because they are Christian; and that the right to choose a place of residence, to enter school, to secure employment, to vote, or attend church should in no way be limited by a person's race or culture, and

WHEREAS the essence of integrity is to demonstrate ideals and not merely talk about them, be it, therefore,

RESOLVED, That the General Assembly of the Church of God in session at Anderson, Indiana, urge its members to take direct action as a religious duty to do their part in their local communities to see that voting, jobs, housing, education, and public worship facilities are available to all citizens, and be it further

RESOLVED, That the Assembly urge each pastor to encourage greater personal involvement on the part of individual Christians in the struggle for racial justice.

65. Stand Against Tobacco

June 1965

WHEREAS we in the Church of God movement have traditionally stood solidly against the use of tobacco in any form and have observed the general undesirability of the habit; and

WHEREAS we observe the vast amounts of money spent for tobacco, which expenditure could not be considered a constructive part of life or a contribution to human welfare; and

WHEREAS we have actively taught that the human body and mind is the temple of God, to be kept clean, pure, and fit for the Master's use; and

WHEREAS we consider it of great importance to protect our youth from the insidious advertising which seems to make the use of tobacco desirable by glamorizing the stars of the entertainment and athletic world; and

WHEREAS the report of the Surgeon General of the United States has injected a decisive, authoritative, and scientifically based analysis showing the harmful effects of tobacco, substantiating what we have long believed to be true, therefore, be it

RESOLVED, That in this General Assembly we reaffirm our convictions and teaching regarding the use of tobacco; be it further

RESOLVED, That this Assembly urge every minister to take a positive stand in discouraging the use of tobacco, to teach constructively, to help safeguard our youth, to help church leaders realize the importance of setting a good example, to lead the church in a redemptive attitude and effort toward those who are victims of the habit; and be it further

RESOLVED, That this General Assembly urge ministers and responsible church laymen to write their Congressmen, calling for stricter regulations on advertising of tobacco in the mass media and on items for sale.

66. Military Conscription: The Right of Conscience

June 1966

Like all true Americans, we as members of the General Assembly of the Church of God meeting in regular session in Anderson, Indiana, this sixteenth day of June, 1966, view with deep concern the escalating military involvement and the conscription of our youth for military service. We believe that war represents our moral failures. We abhor the causes that lead to war. We stand by the teaching and example of our Lord, who taught us and showed us the way of radical, sacrificial love.

We are thankful to God that we live in a land of basic freedoms whose law makes provision for alternative service by those "who, by reason of religious training and belief, are conscientiously opposed to participation in war in any form." We encourage our young men who conscientiously object to war to engage in such civilian work which contributes "to the maintenance of the national health, safety or interest."

We respect the right of each person to arrive at his own convictions. We believe in the principle of freedom of worship and freedom of conscience. We respect the rights of the individual conscience within our fellowship. We have never set up an authoritative creed. Instead, we accept the entire New Testament as our rule of faith and practice, and we seek to lead every member of our fellowship to full comprehension and full acceptance of the Spirit of Christ as the guide for all conduct. What we seek for ourselves we seek for every citizen of our land—the right of individual conscience which no governmental authority can abrogate or violate. We do not condemn or reject that person who differs with our position or participates in war. We shall seek to follow such persons with a ministry of help and guidance, but this is never to be construed as approval of war.

We fervently pray for the leaders of our nation and of other nations, many of whom we believe to be sincerely striving for peace. We pray that efforts by negotiation among countries, through the United Nations, and every possible channel may succeed in bringing peace to our troubled world. Let this statement of conviction be construed by any and all to mean that we fully support young men of the Church of God who sincerely and conscientiously are opposed to participation in military service. We encourage them to seek the constructive alternatives intended to bring health, healing, and understanding, and which serve the highest interests of our beloved country and of the whole world.

67. World Hunger

June 1966

WHEREAS government and relief organizations have been making special studies of world hunger, giving special attention to India and other countries of the Eastern Hemisphere; and

WHEREAS churches and voluntary agencies have been expressing during recent months a mounting concern for the hungry of the world— the two-thirds of the world's population who suffer daily or recurrent hunger; and

WHEREAS the United States government and other world governments have made substantial contributions in recent years and months to supply emergency food commodities to prevent famine and to aid the governments of countries where hunger prevails to use technical skills to produce more and distribute more effectively all available supplies of food; and

WHEREAS for the first time in history the capabilities and techniques exist to prevent the warping of lives and the deaths caused by hunger; and

WHEREAS it should be recognized with regret that the food situation and its distribution around the world are not totally removed from world and local economics and world and local politics; and

WHEREAS united steps are being taken through world relief organizations to attack the long-range problem by caring for emergency feeding operations followed by a mounting aid program to enhance agricultural production, more adequate distribution of processed food, land reclamation, water provision, planned parenthood, and all related issues designed to get at the root causes of world hunger; and

WHEREAS all Christians, particularly those living in affluent societies, are faced with the moral and spiritual responsibility for compassionate action by acknowledging our common humanity and by giving food to the hungry in the name of Christ; be it, therefore,

RESOLVED, That this specter of world hunger be brought to the attention of the Church of God constituency through the medium of this resolution, as well as through current articles appearing in church and secular magazines and in the press; to awaken the conscience of each and every Christian to exert all his energies and to cooperate with efforts to help alleviate world hunger; and be it further

RESOLVED, That in view of the prevailing need in India today caused by the worst drought in seventy years with a resulting 80% to total crop failure in areas hard hit due to lack of monsoon rain, and in view of the possibility that large numbers now suffering from hunger may starve to death unless immediate assistance reaches India quickly; all who wish to respond to this great need and the prompting of their conscience do so by sending their contributions for world relief to the Missionary Board of the Church of God, all monies to be distributed immediately to direct need through Church of God missionaries involved in relief or through Church World Service, the most capable church-related organization to understand and meet the emergency needs found in India and other countries of the world.

68. Racial Justice a Spiritual Priority

June 1968

WHEREAS our Assembly has received various resolutions across recent years concerned about race relations in the Church of God; and

WHEREAS the abundant supply of resolutions on the matter of race relations continues to call attention to our need to correct evident deficiencies and solve evident problems; and

WHEREAS the 1964 Report from this Assembly's Commission on Race Relations stated our deficiencies and recommended appropriate steps for correcting our needs; and

WHEREAS it is the work of this Assembly to authorize, mobilize, and direct the interests common to our life and work as a church—and has effectively done so more recently solving problems of finance (appropriations for college needs, building of Warner Auditorium); and

WHEREAS the church looks to the Assembly to advise and give direction on the particularly spiritual concerns of church life and work; therefore be it

RESOLVED, That this Assembly declare that its previous resolutions on the matter of race relations remain as issues of spiritual priority; and be it further

RESOLVED, That our national boards and agencies be directed to make deliberate moves to secure Negro leaders for executive and/or administrative roles wherever and whenever possible, this being a way to show a more truly inclusive pattern for ourselves on the national level; and be it further

RESOLVED, That this Assembly direct the Commission on Social Concerns to serve the Assembly by preparing such aids and guides for congregational use in resolving differences that keep some of our churchs racially separate; and be it finally

RESOLVED, That this Assembly call upon the Church to repent for the deficiencies and failures as a people on the point of race relations, turning to God for renewal and grace during this International Convention.

69. Resolution on Race

June 1968

In 1957, the Executive Council of the Church of God and the General Ministerial Assembly named a study commission on race relations to serve for a period of five years. In 1961, this study commission reported to the Executive Council and recommended positive strategy for reaching desirable goals in better race relations.

These were:

1. Proceed with all deliberate speed to integrate ratification procedures in all states immediately.
2. Let ministers in all states arrange for fellowship meetings together and pave the way for integrated assemblies, beginning, also, to synchronize meetings, and procedures, adopt similar standards, and so on. Breakfast meetings or one-day prayer retreats might be employed.
3. National leaders should enter into serious discussions toward the integration of national agencies, it being understood that leadership opportunity, representation, and expression would be on the basis of qualification regardless of race.
4. That recognition and support be given to certain experiences and developments which our national boards are carrying out. That encouragement be given to local churches that are able to move ahead with courage in this field, and that these churches on the frontier of exploration be supported with prayer and the concern of the church, and to the churches of the community, whatever the racial situation may be.
5. Let the Executive Council and the General Ministerial Assembly pass resolutions directed to our own churches, urging inter-racial fellowship within the local church and among local churches, asking our people to press forward toward integration on a truly Christian basis.

6. To take a positive stance, by resolution and through publications, on the matter of integration and the employing of our rich traditions and spiritual resources toward the demonstrations of Christian principles at this point of need.
7. That our ministers and churches be encouraged to cooperate in inter-church and community endeavors toward overcoming the racial cleavages.

In 1964, the council offered and this Assembly adopted a further major statement on race, declaring that the urgency for action was growing in society and the need for the church to begin within its own fellowship to make corrections was imperative. Action was called for on the local, the state, and the national levels of our work.

Much progress has been made since these recommendations were adopted. On the local level, a large number of our congregations are now, to some degree, integrated with families of other races. The call for an open-door policy for all races was made but has never been followed up.

On the state level, several assemblies have been merged and others are in the process of merging.

On the national level, there has been a ninety-percent increase in the number of black representatives serving on national boards and agencies. The Missionary Committee of the National Association of the Church of God has been merged with the Missionary Board of this Assembly. The program of the International Convention has become much more representative of all races.

While these gains are encouraging, they have not kept up with the changes in society, the progress is much too slow and the urgency is increasing. There are eleven states which still have two racial ministerial assemblies. Therefore, be it

RESOLVED, That this Assembly urge all state organizations to bring about full involvement and fair representation of Negro persons according to ability in the offices and boards and committees of the state organizations; and be it further

RESOLVED, That where there are Negro and white assemblies still existing, steps be taken in accordance with the recommendations adopted in 1964 to "integrate all ratification procedures in all states immediately"; and be it also further

RESOLVED, That state assemblies report the degree of progress now existing toward integration of assemblies as adopted by this Assembly in 1964, and that the Executive Council, through its Division of Church Service, be instructed to bring to this Assembly in 1969 a summary of the progress that has been made.

70. Open-Door Policy

June 1968

Chairman Boyer recognized Dr. Robert H. Reardon, president of Anderson College. Dr. Reardon referred to Charles Naylor's hymn, "The

Church's Jubilee," and quoted the verse, "Reaching our hands in fellowship to every blood-washed one." He stated that we have in the past expressed an "open-door policy for all races," but there is a need for more positive action. He presented the following resolution, which had been considered by the Business Committee. The committee permitted its presentation.

In view of the open-door resolution passed by this Assembly in 1964, be it

RESOLVED, That this Assembly call upon local congregations of the Church of God in the United States and Canada to ratify the following declaration and to make it known publicly through whatever means possible:

In accordance with the teaching of the Scriptures, this congregation of the Church of God welcomes fellow Christians without regard to race, color, or national origin, to participate fully and without any reservation in its fellowship and work.

And be it further

RESOLVED, That the executive secretary of the Executive Council of the Church of God is instructed to place the above declaration before each local congregation of the Church of God, and to make public those congregations ratifying this declaration.

The Assembly approved this resolution.

71. Conviction on War and Peace

June 1971

Like all true Americans, we as members of the General Assembly of the Church of God meeting in regular session in Anderson, Indiana, this 16th day of June, 1971, view with deep concern the military involvement and the conscription of our youth for military service. We believe that war represents our moral failures. We abhor war and the causes that lead to it. We stand by the teaching and example of our Lord, who taught us and showed us the way of radical, sacrificial love.

We are thankful to God that we live in a land of basic freedoms whose law makes provision for alternative service by those "who, by reason of religious training and belief, are conscientiously opposed to participation in war in any form." We encourage our young men who conscientiously object to war and participation in it to engage in such civilian work which contributes "to the maintenance of the national health, safety or interest."

We respect the right of each person to arrive at his own convictions. We believe in the principle of freedom of worship and freedom of conscience. We respect the rights of the individual conscience within our fellowship. We have not set up an authoritative creed. Instead, we accept the entire New Testament as our rule of faith and practice. We seek to lead every member of our fellowship to full comprehension and full acceptance of the Spirit of Christ as the guide for all conduct. What we seek for ourselves we seek for every citizen of our land—the right of individual conscience which no governmental authority can abrogate or violate.

We believe that the cause of Christ is best served when the Christian of draft age responds freely to his own conscience. Because we believe this, we support those who take the position of the conscientious objector. At the same time we insist that the conscientious military person has similar privileges and responsibilities before God. We also support that person who differs with our position regarding conscientious objectors and participates in military service. We seek to follow all persons with a ministry of help and guidance, but this is not to be construed as approval of war.

We fervently pray for the leaders of our nation and of other nations, many of whom we believe to be sincerely striving for peace. We pray that efforts by negotiation among countries, through the United Nations and every possible channel may succeed in bringing peace to our troubled world. We pray for the Church all over the world to continue her rightful role in peacemaking.

Let this statement of conviction be construed by any and all to mean that we fully support young men of the Church of God who sincerely and conscientiously are opposed to participation in military service. We encourage them to seek constructive alternatives intended to bring health, healing, and understanding, and which serve the highest interests of our beloved country and of the whole world.

72. Refugees

June 1973

RESOLVED, That the General Assembly of the Church of God urge local congregations to search out and discover these refugees and to devise ways and means of meeting their needs by participating with other like-minded groups in discharging a basic biblical imperative, and be it further

RESOLVED, That this resolution and its accompanying document of information be disseminated to state boards of evangelism and to the pastors and official boards of local congregations in the areas where these refugee problems might appear, with an urgent request for serious implementation.

RESOLVED, That the General Assembly of the Church of God urge individuals in congregations to keep currently informed regarding any major refugee situation in the world and how immediate relief and ultimate rehabilitation can be accomplished as the political situation will allow, and that the above information be secured through the Committee on Refugees of the United Nations, Church World Service of the Division of Overseas Ministries of the National Council of Churches, the Missionary Board of the Church of God, or the Executive Council of the Church of God, as well as through the media of the press and news magazines, and be it further

RESOLVED, That the above resolution with the document, "Refugee Settlement: Persons Outside the United States," be sent to all pastors of the Church of God, with the earnest request that the church be encouraged to study it and other available information to the end that it might bring Christian principles governing such matters to the attention of proper governmental authorities, both state and federal, in such a manner that the government and people of the United States might better serve their proper role in the settlement of refugee situations wherever and whenever they might occur.

73. Role of Women

June 1974

The Church of God in its beginning and through its early history included both men and women in its ministry. Little or no thought was given as to whether one who went forth to serve in the name of the Lord Jesus Christ was masculine or feminine. The emphasis was on spreading the gospel of truth as proclaimed by the reformation movement. Women served in many capacities, as evangelists, teachers, musicians, pastors. And they served well along with men down through the years.

A recent survey by the Division of Church Service, through a questionnaire, revealed that while women make up around 55% of the membership of the congregations of the Church of God, the percentage of women in leadership roles has steadily declined.

Therefore, in light of the statistics which document the diminishing use of women's abilities in the life and work of the church, we present the following resolution:

WHEREAS women are equipped by their Creator to serve in a variety of roles including that of homemaker, employment in jobs and professions, volunteer work, and full- or part-time Christian service, and

WHEREAS women have demonstrated their ability and their commitment to the church, and

WHEREAS God calls women to use their gifts and skills to their fullest potential, therefore be it

RESOLVED, That more women be given opportunity and consideration for positions of leadership in the total program of the Church of God, locally, statewide, and nationally.

74. World Hunger

June 1975

WHEREAS Christian people in the wealthy nations, especially Christian people in the United States, should be influential in bringing resources to help alleviate the current world hunger crisis, and

WHEREAS there has been a concern expressed in Church of God periodicals and in mailings from national agencies that feeding starving people should be a top priority of the Church, therefore, be it

RESOLVED, That the church actively seek to raise $100,000 for World

Hunger and Disaster Relief during the year of 1975-76. This effort would include the $25,000 that the WOMEN OF THE CHURCH OF GOD are seeking to raise, the $7,500 listed in the budgets of the Missionary Board and the $20,000 Disaster Fund, leaving $50,000 to be raised by World Service. All money sent to World Service for World Hunger Relief will receive World Service credit.

75. Violence on Television

June 1977

WHEREAS in recent years we have witnessed on television an alarming increase in the use of profanity and violence and the portrayal of life-styles inconsistent with Christian values; and

WHEREAS the television networks and program sponsors have permitted profanity, violence, and the portrayal of life-styles inconsistent with Christian values to be included in an increasing number of telecasts; and

WHEREAS we believe this trend to be detrimental to the well-being of our families—especially our children and youth; therefore, be it

RESOLVED, That the General Assembly of the Church of God, Anderson, Indiana, adopt the following write-in plan to combat the use of profanity and violence and the portrayal of life-styles inconsistent with Christian values on television:

The plan: Each congregation would be asked to appoint a social action chairman (or the pastor may initiate this plan). The chairman (or pastor) would enlist the entire membership locally to write a brief letter to the three network presidents (3 letters) and program sponsors stating their opposition to the use of profanity and violence and the portrayal of lifestyles inconsistent with Christian values on television. This could be done over a period of two or three months. The size of the local congregation would determine how many letters could be assigned for each week.

For example: A church of 100 members would enlist 8 persons each week so that in approximately three months all members would take their turn in writing to the television networks and program sponsors; be it further

RESOLVED, That, if this plan is adopted, the General Assembly, through the Commission on Social Concerns, convey this plan with appropriate publicity to all local congregations, urging that every congregation of the Church of God be enlisted in this action.

76. Stand Against Homosexuality

June 1979

Since the world is invaded by sex perversion in the form of homosexuality, we, the Church of God Reformation Movement, do hereby express our conviction concerning the issue:

67

WHEREAS we in the Church of God, being an evangelical people, committed to biblical holiness, give high regard to scriptural injunctions against homosexuality, we are also a redemptive body and seek to express love, compassion, and a chaste relationship in Christ for everyone; be it

RESOLVED, That the General Assembly of the Church of God go on record as affirming our conviction that biblically we believe homosexuality is sin. We hereby stand firmly opposed to the licensing, ordination, or approving of persons in leadership actively involved in this life-style; be it further

RESOLVED, That we stand opposed to any instruction in our church-sponsored institutions or the use of curriculum material which accepts homosexuality as either normal, desirable, or Christian.

77. Stand Against Abortion on Demand

June 1981

After years of activity in the United States directed at passage of an equal rights amendment (ERA) to the national Constitution and related decisions of the Supreme Court, the General Assembly decided to speak on the major social concern of the legal availability of abortion to almost anyone for almost any reason. The assembly action read:

WHEREAS the United States Supreme Court has declared unconstitutional all state laws regulating abortion, and has opened the way for abortion on demand for any reason; and

WHEREAS the rights of the unborn child are being stripped away by reinterpretation of the Constitution by the Supreme Court; and

WHEREAS this opens the door to possible elimination of other unwanted or undesirable human beings; and

WHEREAS the Bible contains reference to God's personal acquaintance with children prior to birth, inferring the fetus has life, such as

1. In Jeremiah 1:4, 5 ". . . the Word of the Lord came unto me saying, 'Before I formed you in the womb I knew you, and before you were born I consecrated you; I have appointed you a prophet to the nations.' " (NASV);

2. And in Psalm 139:13, King David inspired by God, wrote, "Thou didst form my inward parts; thou didst weave me in my mother's womb. I will give thanks to thee, for I am fearfully and wonderfully made." (NASV); and

WHEREAS abortion on demand, we believe, greatly diminishes the moral values, not only of the one seeking abortion, but of this whole nation; and

WHEREAS the unborn child cannot plead in its own defense; be it, therefore,

RESOLVED, That the General Assembly of the Church of God go on record as opposing abortion on demand, recognizing that the unborn fetus is a living human being and thus should be protected by the laws and Constitution of the United States of America; and be it further

RESOLVED, That the General Assembly of the Church of God urges all congregations to express our compassion and concern not only to protect life before birth but to work to assure that the lives that are preserved may receive the care, attention, and help that God wants for all persons; to provide family life and marriage education that will foster such a reverence for God-given life that both the causes and consequences of unwanted pregnancies may be diminished; and that this resolution be publicized.

78. Nuclear Arms Reductions

June 1982

The incineration of our planet may be imminent! Why? Because of the threat posed by the nuclear arms race in which our country and the Soviet Union are principal participants. Planning the future of our global community is begging the question about a future for this nuclear age. The nuclear arms race itself could end with its destruction of the human race. We believe that the proliferation of nuclear weapons is a sin against the Creator and against His creation.

Because it may be the most urgent moral issue confronting our generation, we call Church of God people everywhere to fast and pray for world peace, and for global leaders as they make decisions which affect the destiny of the human family. We welcome the decision of the United Nations to hold a Second Special Session on Disarmament, and we invite concerned persons and groups to join in fervent prayer during those crucial days. We urge that families, pastors, Sunday school classes, youth, and other groups in local churches give serious study to the question of nuclear disarmament.

We commend the growing number of concerned persons in the Church of God who are expressing opposition to the nuclear arms race in letters to congressmen, senators, elected government leaders, and to local newspaper editors. The positive results of personal letters have been confirmed by both supporters and opponents of nuclear disarmament. We urge that these efforts in sending handwritten letters be continued and accelerated.

The nuclear arms race is not our fate but our choice. There is an alternative. No sinister external force or internal political system is imposing nuclear weapons upon us. Today we are playing brinkmanship with a nuclear shootout because of the accumulation of decisions made by our policy-makers elected and supported by voters and taxpayers. The decision about whether or not we go over the brink into a nuclear holocaust will be made by us, not by persons now in kindergarten, elementary or high school.

The alternative is the way of negotiation and agreement. Just as Mr. Nixon made creative efforts to normalize our relationship with China, and as Mr. Sadat won the admiration of the world when he carried the olive branch to Israel, we call upon Mr. Reagan and Mr. Brezhnev to say to each other and to the people of the world: "Enough of this; let us live in peace."

Our deliberate choice is to be faithful to Jesus Christ and to his gospel of reconciliation. His purpose for all people is life that is abundant and eternal. To place our trust in weapons of mass murder and destruction is irresponsible and idolatrous. We encourage Church of God people to accept our historical imperative to choose life and to find and support alternatives to the nuclear arms race.

Editor's note: The above statement was received rather than formally adopted by the Assembly so that members of the Assembly could feel free to act upon such convictions as they saw fit.

79. Turning the U.S. Back to God

June 1983

WHEREAS it appears that our nation is being confronted with the destruction of the principles upon which it was founded; and

WHEREAS the Declaration of Independence clearly cites "our reliance on the protection of Divine Providence"; and

WHEREAS in many ways the nation's conscience has become insensitive to our reliance on Divine Providence and to the destruction of the moral principles upon which this nation was founded; and

WHEREAS the President of the United States is currently urging the government authorities in this country to permit Bible reading and prayer in the schools and to cease the approval and financing of abortion; and

WHEREAS the Church of God Reformation Movement does not believe in the forbidding of the reading of God's Word or prayer to God in public schools and has gone on record as opposing "Abortion on Demand" (June 1981); be it, therefore,

RESOLVED, That the General Assembly of the Reformation Movement of the Church of God in session at Anderson, Indiana (June 1983), go on record, and so notify the President and the Congress of the United States, that this church body does strongly support the President of the United States, and all concerned members of Congress, in their efforts to turn this country back to God.

80. Pornography and Obscenity

June 1984

WHEREAS the 8-billion-dollar pornography industry in America has grown to epidemic proportions and invaded every segment of society; and

WHEREAS the life-style propagated by the pornographic industry is contrary to the New Testament teachings; and

WHEREAS family, church, and community values are being seriously threatened by the pornography industry; and

WHEREAS the Supreme Court in 1973 reaffirmed the right of the community to protect its standards; and

WHEREAS the erosion of values has contributed to the increase in teen-age pregnancies, child prostitution, and sexual assaults upon women; therefore be it

RESOLVED, That this General Assembly support the Executive Council and the Commission on Social Concerns in their effort to inform our congregations about the seriousness of the problem; and be it further

RESOLVED, That this Assembly designate October 28-November 4 as Pornography Awareness Week issuing a call to decency; and be it further

RESOLVED, That this Assembly request resource packets for our congregations so that they will be equipped to take positive action; and be it further

RESOLVED, That this Assembly urge our congregations to become involved in a plan of action in their own communities as well as using their voice as a positive influence in the media and law; and finally be it

RESOLVED, That this Assembly direct its executive officer to write the President of the United States:

   a. Asking him to make a public declaration that enforcement of the Federal obscenity laws is a matter of importance to him;
   b. Requesting him to order the Justice Department to enforce the obscenity laws which are now on the books;
   c. Pledging him our prayers and support in this effort.

81. Apartheid

June 1986

Jesus demonstrated and taught that we are to love God with all our hearts, souls, minds and strength and to love our neighbor as ourselves. The Good News is that God has reached out to all people with the offer of Salvation and Reconciliation and that we, having become beneficiaries of His grace, become ministers of Reconciliation.

Apartheid, the policy of racial separation in South Africa, obviously violates both the witness and the spirit of God for all people of that nation. Oppression and violence are instruments aligned with Apartheid and are further manifestations of the philosophy of racial superiority. Both in thought and in action, this policy is diametrically opposed to the witness of Christ.

Brothers and sisters of the National Association Ministerial Assembly of the Church of God have eloquently expressed their condemnation of Apartheid. They hold out for us an example of concerned, constructive involvement.

With them, we, the General Assembly of the Church of God, oppose Apartheid in South Africa and all that it implies.

We call upon individuals within the Church to become properly informed so that they might speak, write and act to express their personal disapproval of Apartheid.

Finally, we encourage the Church of God to pledge her support to efforts at reconciliation and peace-making in South Africa.

82. Domestic Violence

June 1986

WHEREAS we recognize that domestic violence is a major problem in the United States today, affecting thousands of families in every economic, social, and ethnic group; and

WHEREAS we believe that awareness of the severity of the problem is the first step in combatting this evil; and

WHEREAS we recognize that misinterpretation of Scripture has permitted some persons to justify domestic violence as being consistent with Christian doctrine; and

WHEREAS we also recognize that breaking the chain of violence is imperative to resolving the problem so that future generations do not perpetuate the evil; therefore, be it

RESOLVED, That we call upon the Church of God Reformation Movement to break the silence barrier on domestic violence by recognizing and addressing the problem within our communities and within our own communion; and be it, also,

RESOLVED, That we urge careful interpretation of Scripture, realizing that correct understanding of the Bible affirms the value and dignity of each individual; and be it, also,

RESOLVED, That we regard violence to be inappropriate as a means of conflict resolution between adult family members; and be it, also,

RESOLVED, That we recognize as unacceptable any behavior that goes beyond normal chastisement measures to use any form of violence in the family that grievously injures, maims, or causes psychological impairment (i.e., severe beatings, kicks, punches, or verbal abuse and depersonalization); and be it, also,

RESOLVED, That we in the church assist persons in our communion to find alternative means of resolving conflict within the family, rejecting completely the practice of violence as defined above; and be it, also,

RESOLVED, That we in the church work to find specific ways to provide protection and healing for the victims of domestic violence; and be it further

RESOLVED, That we also commit ourselves to working for healing for the perpetrators of domestic violence.

83. Nuclear Weaponry

June 1986

We are a biblical people . . .

"The earth is the Lord's and the fullness thereof" (Ps. 24:1).

We are called to stewardship of the earth, and life.
We therefore oppose the use of nuclear weaponry by any nation because it has the capacity to destroy God's creation.

Editor's note: A subsequent motion was passed calling for the above to be sent to the president of the United States and other appropriate government officials.

84. Pornographic Materials

June 1986

WHEREAS there has been a rising tide of pornographic materials made ever increasingly available in the family marketplace of America; and

WHEREAS our movement, through the effective leadership of our Executive Secretary, has taken a leadership role in joining with other concerned persons and groups to raise the standard of decency; and

WHEREAS as a Movement we have historically believed in and attempted to call our world to righteousness; and

WHEREAS we note with thanksgiving that through these united efforts in this battle, we have seen some victories, in that more than 15,000 stores have removed pornographic magazines in the last four months, including such chains as Seven-Eleven Stores, Eckerds Drug Stores, Stop and Go Markets and Super-X Drug stores; and

WHEREAS we are aware that there is still much to be done in the battle to rid our society of this degrading influence; therefore, be it

RESOLVED, That we salute the past efforts of our pastors and leaders who have been involved in this fight against the pornographic tide; and be it further

RESOLVED, That we call upon the Church of God to redouble our efforts to lift up a standard of righteousness and to continue working in cooperation with other like-minded persons and groups until total victory is achieved.

Editor's note: This 1986 action was supplemented in 1990 by the adoption of a vigorous resolution calling for specific actions against illegal pornography, "a dangerous and harmful evil in American society which must be eradicated."

85. Ministry with Older Adults

June 1988

WHEREAS the current United States population of persons 65 and over is now approaching twelve percent (12%) of the total population with future estimates projected to be approximately 20% by the year 2030 A.D.; and

WHEREAS the Bible affirms old age as a time when persons are able to reflect earnestly on their lives, share wise counsel with others and develop the deep spiritual resources of their experiences; and

WHEREAS the Church of God (Anderson, Indiana) has an abundant number of older persons who are able to make significant contributions to their church, community and society; and

WHEREAS because the local church is the center of life for a significant number of older persons who look to the church for spiritual nurture, inspiration and direction; and

WHEREAS the National Board of Christian Education has launched the National Fellowship of Older Adults (N. F. O. A.) and has printed an Older Adult Ministry and Program Manual to assist local church leaders, state/regional organizations to plan and implement effective ministries and programs for older adults; and

WHEREAS Anderson University (School of Theology) has received a grant to train pastors, ministers and other key lay persons in developing their skills to minister more effectively with and to older adults; and

WHEREAS some local congregations, state/provincial/regional organizations and national Church of God agencies have begun to initiate programs for the aged; and

WHEREAS we believe that older persons are an integral part in the life of the Church of God on whom we have been able to build strong and viable congregations; be it, therefore,

RESOLVED, That the General Assembly of the Church of God (Anderson, Indiana) proclaims 1989 as the Year of "Ministry to and with Older Adults"; and be it further

RESOLVED, That pastors, local congregations, state and regional/provincial organizations be encouraged to join in with the National Fellowship of Older Adults, Commission on Social Concerns and national agencies of the Church of God in promoting ministries and programs for and with older persons.

86. Responsible Sexual Behavior

June 1988

WHEREAS forces in society encourage sexual intercourse before marriage; and studies indicate that in society in general, by age nineteen, 80 percent of today's males and 67 percent of today's females are sexually active; and in the United States alone more than 1,000,000 unmarried teen-agers become pregnant every year; and

WHEREAS there is an epidemic of sexually transmitted diseases; and premarital sexual intercourse can damage physical, mental, emotional and spiritual health; and

WHEREAS the home has come under attack on many fronts and the family is struggling against forces greater than those faced by previous generations, and as a result parents are seeking additional knowledge and skills for teaching scriptural principles concerning sexuality, sexual activity, marriage and proper self-image; and

WHEREAS parents and teen-agers desire better communication with one another but may lack the basic skills to accomplish this; and the church, as a basic support group for the family, is called to address and minister to these needs, be it, therefore,

RESOLVED, That the Church of God reaffirm its commitment to the sanctity of marriage and the reserving of sex for marriage; and be it further

RESOLVED, That the Church of God seek to train parents and other significant adults for effectively communicating Biblical principles, especially those related to sexuality, sexual activity, marriage and healthy self-image to young people, and that the Church of God seek to develop among parents, other significant adults, and teen-agers improved relational skills in an atmosphere of love and acceptance; and be it further

RESOLVED, That the above stated goals be addressed at every level and through every avenue of the church's ministry; through national agencies, through provincial, state and regional ministries, through such major gatherings as provincial, state and regional youth conventions and camp meetings, through the Inspirational and International Youth Conventions, and through the local church; and be it further

RESOLVED, That the church avail itself of various excellent resources such as the "WHY WAIT?" materials supplied by Josh McDowell Ministry which have been adopted for use by other evangelical church groups. These materials, having been reviewed by a select group comprised of representatives from the national agencies of the Church, youth ministers and other special interest groups, are considered sound in their content, effective in their usefulness, accurate in their Biblical application, and are recommended for use across the church.

87. Thanksgiving and Responsibility

June 1988

WHEREAS the celebration of a Thanksgiving season has been a national tradition observed by the people of the United States from the days of the early settlers to the present time; and

WHEREAS many of the great leaders of the Nation, including Presidents George Washington and Abraham Lincoln, recognized the importance of setting aside a time of Thanksgiving, and presidential proclamations have established the last Thursday of November as a day of Thanksgiving; and

WHEREAS in 1941, the United States Congress established Thanksgiving as a permanent national holiday; and

WHEREAS we, as a Nation have been blessed above all other nations; and

WHEREAS the United States Constitution has adapted to changing times and is the oldest written constitution in the world; and

WHEREAS the people of the United States should better understand the history of this great Nation; and

WHEREAS it is appropriate to give thanks to God for the everyday freedoms guaranteed by the Constitution that the people of the United States so often take for granted; and

WHEREAS the people of the United States should take time to appreciate a land of plenty, a Nation of vast human and natural resources while not forgetting the plight of the needy; and

WHEREAS the National Thanksgiving Foundation, which has as its purposes: "To promote grassroots and private-sector involvement to help in the elimination of hunger and homelessness and to encourage nationwide expressions of thanksgiving for the blessings of life and liberty in America" is sponsoring simultaneous "National Thanksgiving Dinners" on November 17, 1988 to assist the hungry and homeless; and

WHEREAS the Church of God of Anderson, Indiana supports the objectives of feeding the hungry and housing the homeless as well as being thankful for the blessings of life and liberty in America; therefore be it

RESOLVED, That the Church of God of Anderson, Indiana encourages its members and other groups and organizations to work together on this national celebration by holding National Thanksgiving Dinners or other such activities on November 17, 1988 to give thanks for our blessings and to raise funds to help the less fortunate.

88. Urban Mission of the Church

June 1989

WHEREAS the Census Bureau reports that the U.S.A. is steadily growing more urban and that presently 75 percent of the population now live in metropolitan areas, and that in 1963, it was 63 percent; and

WHEREAS the world is rapidly becoming urban, with projections ranging from one-half to 80 percent of the world's population living in urban places by the year 2000 (83% for the U.S.A. and Canada), depending on how people are counted and how cities are defined; and

WHEREAS the original charter establishing the Board of Church Extension and Home Missions of the Church of God, Inc. (1921) assigns the Board the responsibility, among others, of engaging in urban mission, mentioning specifically encouraging "home missionary work among . . . city slums" and seeking "to establish churches in large cities and strategic centers or other places where work has not yet opened"; and

WHEREAS at the turn of the century the Church of God was intentional in its urban outreach ministry, establishing Missionary Homes as centers of urban evangelism and compassionate ministries in some 42 cities over three decades; and

WHEREAS many Church of God congregations today have moved away from the core city, largely leaving the urban mission of the church to ethnic minority congregations that often face overwhelming needs with impoverished resources, therefore, be it

RESOLVED, That the General Assembly affirm metropolitan/urban areas of the nation, in all their pluralism and problems, to be proper and fitting places for the Church of God to be on mission . . . ; and be it, also, RESOLVED, That the General Assembly go on record as urging:

(1) pastors of local churches to aggressively pursue a course of consciousness raising regarding our Lord's urban mission mandate,

(2) national agencies to target urban mission and city churches in developing resources for ministry within their assignments,

(3) Church of God colleges and the School of Theology to develop core curriculum that will assist students in understanding the city biblically, theologically and missionally; and be it, also,

RESOLVED, That the General Assembly go on record as urging metro area churches to move beyond occasional fellowship and unity meetings to develop active ministry networks (within existing organizational structures) . . . ; and be it further

RESOLVED, That the Board of Church Extension and Home Missions recommends that the General Assembly enthusiastically accept and endorse this resolution on the Urban Mission of the Church of God as in keeping with the National Strategy of Church Planting for the Church of God for the Next Two Decades, approved by the General Assembly in June, 1984.

F. Emphases, Studies, Celebrations

89. Declaration of Seminary Year

June 1960

WHEREAS this General Ministerial Assembly, upon the recommendations of the Budget Committee of the Executive Council and the Division of World Service, did last year in its June 1959 Assembly, designate the Special Project for the year 1960-61 to be the raising of $100,000 toward the erection of the first unit of the School of Theology building, and

WHEREAS during the year 1960-61, when the campaign to raise this $100,000 will be in progress, those in charge of raising the fund wish to designate the year as SEMINARY YEAR IN THE CHURCH OF GOD, in order to focus the attention of the entire church upon the importance of training our young people for the Church of God ministry, be it

RESOLVED, That the General Ministerial Assembly hereby adopts the following proclamation:

To Every Member of the Church of God, Greetings:

Be it known that the General Ministerial Assembly of the Church of God and its several agencies hereby proclaim the year 1960-1961 as Seminary Year, during which time a special fund of $100,000 shall be raised for the erection of the first unit of the School of Theology building in Anderson, Indiana, for the training of ministers for the

Church of God. Every congregation is urged to study this need and make provision to contribute toward this important work of the Church.

90. Greetings to Zurich World Conference

June 1967

In this 49th General Assembly of the Church of God, convened for the purpose of conducting the business of the Church, and the 78th International Convention, we as ministers and laymen pause to acknowledge our brethren in all countries of the world. We especially send greetings to you who are attending the Fourth World Conference in Zurich, Switzerland.

We feel a bond of love for you which is stronger than the tensions, misunderstandings, and estrangements which are so common between nations and cultures. The work of God in Christ has made us brothers and fellow workers.

The Assembly by a standing vote expresses to you its deepest Christian love and warmest fellowship. We live in a troubled and explosive world. Poverty, hunger, disease, illiteracy, social inequality, and rebellion are a part of our times. We pledge our faithful stewardship and cooperation with our brethren throughout the world in endeavoring to bring the peace of Christ and his deliverance, never letting up on the elimination of these evils.

While you are gathered in Zurich we pray that the Holy Spirit will be real to each of you and that he will bring a flowing together of hearts so that you will truly experience fellowship at the deepest levels.

Where possible we ask that delegates take our greetings and Christian love to the church in their home country.

It was moved, seconded (Charles Weber-Albert Donaldson), and carried by a standing vote that these greetings be conveyed to the Fourth World Conference of the Church of God, Zurich, Switerland.

91. Declaring a Year of Evangelism

June 1970

WHEREAS the Church of God has been invited to participate in the projected 1973 nationwide evangelism thrust, along with other religious communions; and

WHEREAS the Board of Church Extension and Home Missions has offered its services in initiating the 1973 evangelism emphasis for the Church of God; and

WHEREAS the Division of General Service sees great value in a carefully planned emphasis on evangelism, which will bring together interested agencies of the Church in a coordinated effort; and

WHEREAS the Division of General Service has given its enthusiastic endorsement to the projected program and encourages the Board of

Church Extension and Home Missions to initiate the planning, involving all interested agencies of the Church of God, for our participation in the Year of Evangelism Emphasis,

RESOLVED, That the Executive Council designate 1973 as the Year of Evangelism Emphasis, and that it seek the concurrence of the General Assembly by resolution seeking its approval and support by urging each minister and each local congregation of the Church of God to cooperate fully in this program.

Mr. Chairman, since this resolution requests the concurring support of the, General Assembly the Executive Council presents the following motion: be it

RESOLVED, That we, the members of the General Assembly, do hereby concur in the action taken previously by the Division of General Service and the Executive Council in regard to the 1973 Nationwide Evangelism Thrust; and be it further

RESOLVED, That we pledge our enthusiastic cooperation in this concerted effort to make the Christian witness more vital and relevant in American society.

92. Call for a Consultation on Doctrine

June 1970

The General Assembly sessions this year have helped us not only to see and handle our duties but also see and know our strong differences of opinion. Many of the expressed differences concern agency programs and decisions that were vigorously debated against.

WHEREAS some of the expressed differences reflected a possible problem of attitudes as well as opinions; and

WHEREAS many of the differences reflect theological and doctrinal problems that need to be openly and honestly faced by this Assembly; and

WHEREAS some of these problems grow out of evidently changing patterns of our preaching, teaching, and publications across several decades; therefore, be it

RESOLVED, That we urge a serious restudy of the theological and doctrinal message of our Movement; and that the Executive Council and the Graduate School of Theology examine the feasibility of calling a Consultation on Doctrine to allow mutual discussion among us as leaders in faith and practice.

The intent is not to prepare a creed or definitive statement of our position, but rather to hear and examine anew the doctrinal concerns that are important to our life and work as a movement.

Editor's note: For a review of the process that followed passage of the above resolution and a summation by Dr. W. E. Reed of the useful purposes eventually served, see pages 527-31 of *The First Century*, Volume II, by Barry L. Callen (Anderson, Indiana, Warner Press, 1979).

93. Plan for a Centennial Celebration

June 1972

WHEREAS the Church of God, with general agencies in Anderson, Indiana, and with congregations in forty or more countries of the world, will reach its centennial at the end of this decade; and

WHEREAS the Church of God around the world will want to celebrate its centennial in a way that pays tribute to those who have preceded us in this work and, at the same time, present an appropriate challenge to those in generations to come; therefore be it

RESOLVED, That the General Assembly, on this 21st day of June, 1972, concur in the recommendation of its Executive Council in confirming the time period for the Centennial Celebration as beginning with June 1980, and extending through October 1981; and be it further

RESOLVED, That the Executive Council be instructed to proceed through its committee on planning for an observance of the centennial in a manner commensurate with our spiritual heritage and our unrealized hopes.

94. Call for Emphasis on Church Growth

June 1976

WHEREAS there is a continuous need for the Church of God to urgently and aggressively address its attention and resources toward a more adequate fulfillment of the commission given by Jesus Christ to His church, and

WHEREAS in the last few years, there has developed a wide range of tools, techniques, and methods for stimulating church growth, and

WHEREAS we believe God by His Holy Spirit is prompting the Church of God to intensify its efforts in a major evangelistic effort to win new persons to meaningful discipleship, therefore be it

RESOLVED, That the General Assembly of the Church of God, meeting in June 1976, go on record, and hereby do, as endorsing a major effort within the church to stimulate church growth, and be it further

RESOLVED, That:

1. Such a church growth effort be launched July 1, 1978, and continue through June 1980, in the midst of our centennial celebration, and that the program for church growth be designed and administered by a strategy committee as named earlier in this report;

2. The passage of this resolution mandates and pledges wholehearted support on the part of all national agencies of the Church of God in the United States of America for full cooperation and participation in a united effort for church growth;

3. The costs of this effort—as determined by the Strategy Committee— shall be funded through the budget of the Division of General Service by a grant approved by the Budget Committee, and included in the 1977-78 World Service Budget;

4. Members of the General Assembly who vote for this Resolution also pledge their full support to utilize the ministry and tools produced by the Strategy Committee for their congregations and areas;
5. The Strategy Committee will bring to this Assembly in June 1977, a progress report on its work to date, and in June 1978, the committee will bring a report setting forth specific and detailed goals for congregations, state and area assemblies, and national agencies, and a follow-through plan for reaching the projected goals;
6. The Division of General Service will bring to the 1981 General Assembly a summarization report on the effectiveness and accomplishments of the church effort.

95. Prayer and Plans for the 1980 World Conference

June 1977

WHEREAS it is the judgment of this Executive Council and General Assembly that immeasurable good has occurred as the result of the several World Conferences of the Church of God that have been conducted over the past several years; and

WHEREAS the different World Conferences have had a unifying effect upon the Church of God in many different nations and have served to clarify our thinking on many crucial issues to broaden our understanding and appreciation for persons in the Church of God in other parts of the world; and

WHEREAS this Assembly has in many ways across many years given strong encouragement and support to the development of the several World Conferences; therefore, be it

RESOLVED, That this Assembly extend to the World Conference of the Church of God a warm, cordial invitation to have the 1980 World Conference of the Church of God in Anderson, Indiana, in conjunction with the Annual Convention of the Church of God in June of 1980; and be it further

RESOLVED, That we instruct the executive secretary of the Executive Council to carry our Christian greetings and assurance of prayer and support to delegates meeting in the Strategy and Planning Consultation to be held October 17-26, 1977, in Nairobi, Kenya, East Africa; and be it further

RESOLVED, That we express our corporate concern for the success of this consultation and our promise of prayer for the guidance of the Holy Spirit by a standing vote of affirmation.

96. Goal-Oriented Plan for the Future

June 1983

During 1983 final plans were being made for the major Consultation on Mission and Ministry scheduled for April 1984. Many members of the

Assembly were concerned about the Church of God's not seeming to have a definite sense of direction as it prepared to move into the final years of the century. They also were hopeful that the substantial effort being invested in this coming consultation would result in more than a few generalizations that would not focus and energize the movement's ministries. A motion, therefore, emerged from the Assembly floor calling upon the coming consultation to work toward a specific goal-oriented plan for the coming years in the life of the Church of God. The Assembly adopted this motion. (For results of this consultation, see entry 111.)

97. Church Planting

June 1984

WHEREAS God has richly blessed the Church of God reformation with substantial congregational growth through the first century of existence; and

WHEREAS the General Assembly has established the Board of Church Extension and Home Missions to develop and provide services; and

WHEREAS there is an urgent need for a more intensified effort in planning new churches among the Hispanics, Asians, Africans, Arabs and more than 80 million unchurched Americans; and

WHEREAS states and districts have assemblies, officers, state coordinators and Boards of Church Extension and Kingdom Builders to help do church planting and congregational revitalization; and

WHEREAS the state coordinators, the National Board of Church Extension and Home Missions and the National Board of Christian Education have cooperated in selecting a State/National Task Force to seek ways to increase the planting of new churches; therefore, be it

RESOLVED, That the General Assembly recognize and affirm:

That the Church is most obedient to her calling when reaching the lost and unchurched of our nation and world;

That planting and nurturing new churches is Biblical and an effective way to evangelize the lost;

That the ministry and support of church planting, as being done by state and district Boards of Church Extension and Kingdom Builders, continue to be done;

That there is a need for each indigenous congregation to consider sponsoring a new church; and,

That some persons are called and gifted as leaders for starting new churches and that they be urged to cooperate with a state and district Board of Church Extension and Kingdom Builders. And be it further

RESOLVED, That we recommend the General Assembly enthusiastically accept and endorse the National Strategy of Church Planting for the Church of God in North America for the next two decades as one of the major recommendations, goals and ministries for the Church of God.

Editor's note: In the 1988 assembly it was reported that since the 1984 action 106 new congregations of the Church of God had been launched. They were located in 36 different states or districts, representing a good beginning to a central and longterm task. See entry 105.

98. Declaration of a "Year of the Hispanics"

June 1984

WHEREAS there has been a great influx of Hispanics in the 1970s and 80s, principally in the southwest portion of the United States and in all major metropolitan areas, and

WHEREAS Hispanic people constitute one of the largest and most rapidly growing minority groups in the United States, and

WHEREAS an urgent need exists to evangelize and minister in Christian love to these new immigrants of Hispanic origin, and

WHEREAS the Church of God is in a special position of responsibility and opportunity to broaden and increase its growing ministry among Hispanics, and

WHEREAS there is great need to become better acquainted with Hispanic culture and language and to celebrate their contribution to the Church of God, and

WHEREAS the Board of Church Extension and Home Missions meeting in its annual session the 26th day of April 1984, recommended to the Executive Council that 1986 be recognized by the reformation movement as a time for special attention focused upon the Hispanic community, and

WHEREAS the Executive Council concurred in its meeting on May 10, 1984, therefore, be it

RESOLVED, That the General Assembly designate 1986 to be celebrated as the Year of the Hispanics and encourage general agencies and state organizations of the church to find ways to evangelize and minister within Hispanic communities.

99. Year of the Sunday School

June 1987

Editor's note: In grateful recognition of the two hundred years of significant ministry of the Sunday school movement, the Board of Christian Education and the Publication Board jointly sponsored the following, which was affirmed gladly by the General Assembly.

WHEREAS the Sunday school is a vital outreach and nurturing arm of the Church of God; and

WHEREAS the Sunday school provides regular opportunity for teachers and learners to study the Bible for discovering God's instruction for contemporary living; and

WHEREAS the Sunday school provides a time and a setting for unified and systematic study of Church of God doctrine and heritage throughout the Movement; and

WHEREAS the Sunday school represents a rich history of strong lay involvement, enlisting the largest group of volunteer workers in the church; and

WHEREAS the Sunday school provides opportunities for the training and development of leadership in the church; and

WHEREAS the Sunday school is a basic component to church planting and growth strategies; therefore, be it

RESOLVED, That all agencies and congregations of the Church of God give support to the Sunday school and its leaders by declaring September, 1987 through August, 1988 to be The Year of the Sunday School; be it further

RESOLVED, That each congregation set September 13 as the date for launching of the Sunday school year; and be it further

RESOLVED, That we support the Sunday school through the use of "Journey with the Word" curriculum for the Church of God; and be it further

RESOLVED, That we enlist our Sunday schools in the Decade for Sunday School Development; and be it further

RESOLVED, That we emphasize the Sunday school through church growth and planting strategies.

100. Year of Revival in the Church of God

June 1987

WHEREAS the forces of Satan and sin continue their destructive assaults against the cause of Christ; and

WHEREAS the Scriptures teach that true spiritual revival in the Body of Christ will not only restore God's blessing, power and healing to the Church, but will also bring "Healing to the Land," that has become sick unto death; be it, therefore,

RESOLVED, That the Executive Council of the Church of God designate as soon as possible, hopefully 1988-89, a "Year of Revival"; and be it further

RESOLVED, That the International Convention Program Committee for that year consider focusing on the "Revival" theme; and be it further

RESOLVED, That this resolution be sent to each and every national agency and that these agencies be encouraged to pick up on this emphasis in their planning and publications; and be it finally

RESOLVED, That during this time particular emphasis be given to the ministry of intercessory prayer and fasting.

101. Day of Prayer and Fasting

June 1987

WHEREAS there are many kinds of pressures that all persons, clergy and laity, face as they minister in the Kingdom of God; and

WHEREAS there is much disorientation about the morality, testimony, and life-style of Christians currently being witnessed by the world; and

WHEREAS there is such an obvious need to reach this continent and the world for Jesus Christ; and

WHEREAS the leadership needs of the church are so very great (the New Testament Church provides our example, see Acts 13:2-3); and

WHEREAS the ministry opportunities to affect the spiritual and moral destiny of many people are numerous; and

WHEREAS the Bible tells us that "our struggle is not against flesh and blood, but against the rulers, against the authorities, against the powers of this dark world and against the spiritual forces of evil in the heavenly realms" (Ephesians 6:12) and we need divine help to stand; therefore, be it

RESOLVED, That the first Wednesday of each month during the 1987-88 fiscal year be a Day of Prayer and Fasting; and,

RESOLVED, That every congregation of the Church of God be encouraged to promote and observe this Day of Prayer and Fasting; and

RESOLVED, That this program be administered by the office of the Executive Secretary of the Executive Council of the General Assembly of the Church of God; and

RESOLVED, That this observance begin July 1, 1987.

102. The Year of Christian Higher Education

June 1988

Refer to entry 54 for the content of this resolution highlighting the ministry of higher education in the life of the church.

103. Year of Canadian-United States Partnership in Ministry

June 1988

WHEREAS the Church of God in Canada has always been an integral partner in fulfilling the mission of the Church of God Reformation Movement in North America; and

WHEREAS the population of Canada is approaching 30 million people comprised of many socio-ethnic cultures; and

WHEREAS the nation of Canada has ten provinces and two territories with the Church of God having 53 congregations located in six provinces; and

WHEREAS the Canadian Church of God has established and supported the Christian higher educational institution, Gardner Bible College, to prepare laity and pastors for ministry and service, and has contributed numerous missionaries who have served in overseas assignments with the Missionary Board of the Church of God; and

WHEREAS an urgent need exists to evangelize and plant congregations of the Church of God in Canada; and

WHEREAS there is a great need to become better acquainted with Canadian congregations, and to recognize their contribution to the Church of God; and

WHEREAS it is desirable to strengthen cooperation, improve relationship, and foster interdependence between the Church in the United States and Canada; therefore, be it

RESOLVED, That the two Canadian Assemblies along with the General Agency of the Board of Church Extension and Home Missions, Anderson, Indiana, recommend that the Year 1990 be recognized by the Church of God in North America as a time to better understand the need and opportunities to evangelize and plant churches in the nation of Canada; be it further

RESOLVED, That the General Assembly designate 1990 as the Year of Canadian—United States Partnership in Ministry and encourage general agencies, state and area assemblies, and congregations to build supporting relationships with Canadian churches.

104. National Association's Diamond Jubilee

June 1991

WHEREAS the National Association of the Church of God with offices in West Middlesex, Pennsylvania had its inception in August, 1917 when a group of saints, known as "The Brothers and Sisters of Love," held their first camp meeting in West Middlesex, Pennsylvania; and

WHEREAS the National Association (here and after identified by NA) since its beginnings 75 years ago has grown from a small farming community with rolling hills and wooded land to a camp ground site with modern cottages, retreat and recreational facilities and buildings with an assessed evaluation of more than two million dollars; and

WHEREAS the primary motive in starting the NA was a desire of "The Brothers and Sisters of Love," for fellowship with those who believed in and practiced holiness; and

WHEREAS the pioneers of the NA had no intent to start a schismatic movement apart from the international work of the Church of God in Anderson, Indiana, but rather to meet the needs among the Black saints for worship, fellowship and service and to enlist and develop its people without racist overtones and segregation control; and

WHEREAS the NA is a vital and significant organization in the life of the Church of God and continues to make valuable contributions to the national and international life and ministries of the Church of God; and

WHEREAS the impact and influence of the NA upon the Black community of the Church of God has been significant and immeasurable in terms of its scope and ministry, and constituency in the urban centers of our nation; and

WHEREAS the NA has served as a catalyst for social change and cohesion to a significant number of the Black constituency of the Church of God and, at the same time, the NA has raised the social and political consciousness of the Church resulting in some positive changes in race relations, employment, and attitudes; be it, therefore,

RESOLVED, that the 1991 General Assembly of the Church of God join the NA in celebrating its Diamond Jubilee by encouraging local congregations, state and regional assemblies, and national agencies to participate in the week-long celebration scheduled to take place during the Annual Campmeeting at West Middlesex, Pennsylvania, August 11-18, 1991; and be it, therefore,

RESOLVED, That all local, state, and national Church of God publications be encouraged to promote the NA Diamond Jubilee Celebration in their newsletters, magazines and other appropriate publications; be it further

RESOLVED, That this assembly declare August, 1991 to July, 1992 as the year of the NA throughout the Church of God; be it, also,

RESOLVED, That all pastors and congregations be encouraged to acquire and read the NA's Diamond Jubilee Historical Publication; be it finally

RESOLVED, That local congregations, regional and state assemblies, and the national agencies join in partnership with the NA to seek ways to evangelize the world, seek to solve racial problems, resolve church conflict, empower the poor and disadvantaged and utilize our material and human resources for the up-building of the Kingdom of God.

105. Vision 2 Grow!

June 1991

Rationale:

Jesus Christ, our Savior and Lord, commanded,
"Go therefore and make disciples of all nations, baptizing them in the name of the Father and of the Son and of the Holy Spirit, and teaching them to obey everything that I have commanded you" (Matthew 28:19-20 NRSV);

The Mission Statement of the Church of God affirms that we seek "to enable persons . . . to experience the redemptive love in its fullest meaning through the sanctifying power of the gospel and know Jesus Christ as Savior, Master and Lord";

In the nineties, looking forward to the next century, by faith and vision we believe:

—The Church of God has an opportunity to grow, to win more persons to Christ and help them find their place in the fellowship and ministry of a local church;

—Visionary, courageous, and trained pastoral and lay leadership can be enlisted and are essential to growth;

—The Spirit of God is convicting persons of sin and calling the church to be intensely involved in ministries of evangelism and to meet other human needs;

—The rapid change in the structures of society and in culture provides the church with a unique opportunity to proclaim and demonstrate the gospel.

Goals:

1. Church Growth—The Charge for The Future!

In response to the Great Commission, and in recognition of God's desire to increase the Church, we seek to:

A. Plant 60 new congregations each year.
B. Increase U.S. A.M. worship attendance to 200,000 by 1995 and to 225,000 by 2001 with similar growth in Canadian churches.
C. Renew Biblical foundations, strengthen the family, and provide avenues for spiritual maturity.
D. Strengthen congregational response to world need.
E. Target 15 pastors of growing congregations to serve as partners in developing Vision 2 Grow! strategies.

2. Leadership
In response to the need for effective and visionary lay and clergy leadership we seek to:

A. Establish an intentional and focused effort for recruiting ministers.
B. Strengthen present tracks of ministerial enlistment training.
C. Create alternate models for in-service training and support.
D. Challenge and enable pastors and lay persons to:
    (1) Provide visionary leadership
    (2) Exercise their unique gifts
    (3) Be faithful to the trust placed in them

Editor's note: In earlier years other Assembly actions had focused on similar concerns. See entries 91, 94, and 97.

Section III

Churchwide Consultations

A. All Board Congress and Planning Council

B. Consultation of the Church of God

C. Yokefellow Statement

D. Dialogue I on Internal Unity

E. Dialogue II on Internal Unity

F. Consultation on Mission and Ministry

A. All Board Congress and Planning Council

106. All Board Congress and Planning Council

1963

The following is excerpted from the final report of the Findings Committee of the All Board Congress and Planning Committee, 1963.

On April 30—May 2, 1963, an All Board Congress and Planning Council of the Church of God was convened in Anderson, Indiana, to facilitate and focus wide discussion on crucial issues then being faced by the movement as a whole. Some 260 persons participated in this intense and searching experience, including all national board members, selected national staff persons, all full-time state coordinators, and one representative from each state. In October 1963, the Findings Committee of the congress summarized the results as follows:

We call for a clearer, more relevant expression of the existing theological foundations upon which this movement stands. We see the need for a rebirth of doctrinal emphasis, starting with the pulpit ministry and extending through all phases of the Church's life. Such a rebirth, we feel, should be undergirded in our educational work by clearly stated expressions of our faith published in readily available forms and appropriate for our people of all ages and at all stages of their Christian development.

We are discontented with where we have now arrived in the promulgation of our doctrinal position and see the need constantly to call up our teachings for reevaluation, particularly to see how they communicate living truth centered in a living Christ. In this way and through constant vigilance we would hope to avoid arriving at a dry and rigid creedalism which would undermine individuals whose faith is growing in an atmosphere of Christian fellowship and freedom under God. Serious theological discussion should be carried forward.

We recognize the need to maintain and build up a greater sense of unity among ourselves, achieving better and more harmonious working relationships. Our witness must begin with a more adequate demonstration of what we teach.

We recognize that we are not alone in our concern for unity. We have found, in working with our fellow Christians of other groups, kindred minds and spirits. We feel the need to increasingly express toward others the unity we teach, extending the loving fellowship and remembering that this is the basis of unity rather than intellectual uniformity.

While we feel the need to cooperate with other Christian groups, we are not looking toward mergers. We feel the need for more serious study on unity, perhaps by a duly appointed commission, which would find ways to enter into more serious dialogue with our Christian brethren. We must maintain the polarity of our position, expressing it more adequately and clearly while, at the same time, accepting our brethren as equals and as Christians.

To seek distinctiveness as a kind of denominational rationale is unjustifiable. At the same time, a genuine demonstration of Christian unity and of vital personal experience is an invaluable contribution in today's Christendom. If we are to make any distinctive contribution, we want to make sure it is of this kind. Perhaps any distinction should lie precisely in not setting up distinctives in the denominational sense.

We feel that our openness toward fellow Christians and to the truth, our conception of membership by salvation, the absence of creedalism, and our emphasis upon the dynamic nature of living relationships in Christ offer us some opportunity for Christian witness. It may be that our combination of teachings is significant, unity being possible only on the basis of truth and experience emphasized in this movement across the years.

As a church we need to know who we are, and why we are. It is possible to live on the memory of a few strong personalities who were able to rally a good force about them and make the mistake of taking their concepts of truth and attempting to confront today's situations with them. We may be united to one another and our rich heritage rather than united in Christ. We dare not become so preoccupied with ourselves that we feel that we must grow as a movement, forgetting that our mission may be to permeate society as others are doing, as leaven that will benefit the whole loaf.

We register much concern that in the midst of our day-to-day ministry, in the press of pushing a program here and a project there, we have not given enough thought and prayer to developing and keeping sight of great, overarching goals. We feel our need of these to steer our everyday operations, to coordinate our efforts and measure our progress, and to draw us on as we take a long view of all the work that lies before us. We look toward such goals as means of helping us gain an enlarging sense of mission. Only in the light of such clearly defined major goals can we wisely discern the specific objectives we need to set before us. The big goals should not just lie in the haze of the horizon but should be clearly drawn and carefully communicated.

A great theology, clearly understood, and great overarching goals, clearly conceived, mean little in themselves unless they are carefully harnessed to help the Church and its people carry forward significant ministry. We call for an increasingly adequate structure to serve as a channel for implementing our mission. We see a need for a broad study of national, state, and local structure in order to strengthen the work of the Church at every level in a coordinated way. We feel that increased lay representation is called for at all levels.

We saw the need for strong local fellowships of the people of God to be of fundamental importance to the witness and outreach of the movement. Our total evangelistic thrust, our general sense of mission, our missionary out-reach demand strong local congregations.

The fact that a large percentage of our churches are perennially small, weak, and apparently lacking in resources to produce growth, was seen by the congress to be a paramount concern.

91

The need to strengthen leadership, both layman and pastor, was felt to be of central importance. A better understanding of the autonomy of the local church was considered of basic importance. How can this freedom be used wisely in matters of congregational discipline, interpersonal relationships, seeking counsel, and the acceptance of guidance in choosing pastoral leadership?

We recognize the disturbing fact that the pastoral image needs upgrading, both within the Church and in our culture, that frequently the "parson" is no longer the important leader in the community, that often neither the man nor his congregation are thought to be of real importance in the community. There is need to face openly the relationship of "educational attainment" and the image of the pastor. There is need to understand the forces in society which help to create anti-clergy attitudes.

We recognized the growing and valuable role of our seminary in both the enlistment and training of pastors. Closer communication between the seminary and the local church and state-level organizations was seen as desirable.

Some means of in-service training for pastors was recommended. Continued, strengthened, and improved services on the part of the Division of Church Service was encouraged. Stronger state-level organization and better means of examining candidates as well as establishing higher standards of registration and ordination are desirable.

There is a strong feeling among us that we must seek and find a deep spiritual renewal if we are to find adequate motivation for the task ahead. It is not always more knowledge, better techniques, better training, or more tools we need—most of our people know more now than they are willing to use. There is definite agreement that we must cease striving for status or respectability as a church and return to a love for people that constrains us to give ourselves in Christian service because we care about the spiritual, physical, and social needs of others. This also will lead the church to be passionately concerned about winning others to Christ.

Evangelism is seen to be at the very heart of the Church. However, it is obvious that we are not getting the message to enough people fast enough. While in the early years of our movement we grew very rapidly, we seem to be settling down to the way of least resistance.

Major concern has been expressed regarding our knowledge of the world and its needs. Sometimes the sickness of the world communicates itself to the Church more than the Church communicates its life-giving message to the world. It would seem that we are using the language and meanings of another day to communicate with a modern and fast-moving generation. We need to say the same old message in new and different terms or at least bring this generation of new Christians up to date on our language.

We confronted the pressing need to involve the total ministries of the church, the need for full recognition of the scriptural concept of these ministries, and that of heightening the interest of the whole church in the so-called "lay ministries" beyond the usual "church work." A clarification of the lay and pastoral ministries is needed. Various kinds of preparation and training are needed to prepare the church to receive and adequately demonstrate the gifts of the Spirit in the total ministries of the church. We need a strong emphasis on redemptive fellowship in the church. Often our acceptance of other denominations and even members of our own congregations has been conditional, based on whether or not they agreed with "Church of God" thinking. Perhaps we have forgotten the great inclusiveness of "being in Christ." People are going to church where they can receive help, healing, comfort, as well as where they can hear the Truth preached. We need to be mindful of the needs of the total man.

It would seem that our ministry must be concerned with local, state, national, and even international problems of a social nature. Sometimes the ministry of the Church is not appreciated because we have seemingly closed our eyes to situations which exist, such as racial segregation, and so on. We have not been without our own problems as a movement. Perhaps we need to spend time and prayer eliminating our own problems before we talk too loudly.

B. Consultation of the Church of God

107. Consultation of the Church of God

1970

The 1970 Consultation of the Church of God was constituted much like the one in 1963 (see entry 106) with representation from the general agencies and from the state assemblies. It met with full awareness of the 1963 congress, the findings of that meeting having been widely distributed and discussed and the delegates having been given a review of those actions which were taken to implement the findings.

An opening presentation of "the state of the church" suggested three focal points to keep in mind during the discussions:

1. The scriptural and theological base and imperative inhering in the mighty act of God through Jesus Christ which gives the church its very life.
2. The social and practical reality of our time when people are hurting and lost and when Christians are called to incarnational involvement.
3. The relative, and changing position of the Church of God movement within Christendom as it is expressed in fellowship and united witness.

The major work of the consultation was to be done in six sections. The six areas were: (1) Social Concerns, (2) Unity, (3) Lay Ministry, (4) Evangelism, (5) Missions, (6) Leadership. Coordinators had been appointed for each area and asked to prepare "projections" for that section as a basis of study, analysis, and evaluation. Each section had three work groups with sharing times among the groups. Following are some of the issues addressed and the consensus reached. Coordinators were responsible to report the findings and "reflections" from their sections.

1. Social Concerns

Issues: (1) What balance of social and individual emphasis? (2) How can we make the gospel relevant to all persons? (3) How can the church minister effectively in missions, evangelism, unity, and so on, without seriously undertaking to bring reconciliation and equality within its own ranks?

Consensus: (1) Initiate creative programs relating to social concerns and encourage church agencies to do more. (2) Anticipate and plan rather than merely read; help black churchmen prepare for primary executive positions in the church. (3) Redefine and strengthen role in eliminating racism. (4) Disseminate success experiences in elimination of barriers. (5) Actively support churches and pastors who are attempting to overcome racism. (6) Develop and circulate courses of study setting forth biblical imperatives in social concerns. (7) Become a catalyst, prompting churches and pastors in programs of action. (8) Executive Council should clarify the function of the Commission on Social Concerns, giving it economic support and administrative integrity. (9) Continue dialogue between white and black churchmen that goes beyond polite conversation.

2. Christian Unity

Issues: (1) Where is the Spirit leading us in intra- and interchurch unity in the 1970s? (2) What is the nature of the unity we seek? (3) What opportunities and obstacles to unity confront the movement? (4) How can the Church of God best contribute to the ecumenical movement?

Consensus: (1) Polarities recognized were: inclusive vs. exclusive fellowship; social concerns vs. evangelism; "come-outism" vs. cooperative involvement; cardinal beliefs vs. tradition; diversity vs. uniformity; delegated assembly vs. general assembly. (2) Recognition of racial divisiveness and need to press for the removal of it. (3) Need to rethink sainthood and servanthood. (4) Find ways to utilize larger variety of ministries. (5) Remain a non-joiner but initiate more conversations with other groups. (6) Clarify responsibilities of the Committee on Christian Unity. (7) Officially endorse cooperative endeavors overseas. (8) Share insights on unity wherever doors are open.

3. Lay Ministry

Issues: (1) How can laymen best be supported in their own call and ministry in the everyday world? (2) What kind of training do laymen need to maximize their opportunities? (3) How can we broaden our base of planning and strategy to allow for their active participation at the planning, decision-making level?

Consensus: (1) Laymen do want to be significantly involved in the decision-making process. (2) Pastors should see their role more as opening up opportunities and giving guidance rather than trying to do everything themselves. (3) Institutes for laymen on college campuses for task-oriented study are needed. (4) Training institutes of longer duration for retired persons could prepare them for full or part-time leadership. (5) Study should be given to ordaining for lay ministries and the relation of that to baptism. (6) Lay ministry should be more than merely assisting in some "church work"; it should help them identify their own authentic call and support them in it.

4. Evangelism

Issues: (1) Are we an evangelistic people or have we gained mostly by those coming from other groups? (2) Are our methods of evangelism largely pulpit-centered and adequate for today and tomorrow? (3) What is evangelism; what are the essential ingredients? (4) Can we distinguish between personal evangelism and "gimmickry?" (5) Is our structure conducive and adequate for effective evangelization?

Consensus: (1) Admit we have not been very evangelistic and need to seriously address this lack. (2) An evangelistic church is one characterized by warm fellowship, effective preaching, involvement with people and community, and a practical program of evangelistic outreach. (3) The time is overdue for evangelism as the primary thrust of the church. (4) Techniques of some interdenominational groups could well be utilized. (5) Special attention should be given to the inner city.

5. Missions

Issues: (1) With the rapidly changing scene in other countries as well as our own, how can we better address the total task? (2) How can we achieve wider understanding and more informed cooperation in the church? (3) How can we best coordinate existing interest in the church and deploy it in a manner consistent with sound missionary policy? (4) What employment should be made of experienced (perhaps retired) people for specialized needs?

Consensus: (1) Schools are vital on the mission fields; perhaps some relocation is advisable. (2) Missions should be approached on an international basis, perhaps through some kind of international board. (3) Lay people, with orientation and training, should be used at strategic places. (4) There is need for skilled staff personnel in securing large gifts. (5) Missions conventions should be encouraged and guided by the Missions Board. (6) Active recruitment of youth for missionary work is needed. (7) Missionary work means sharing in the ghetto as well as overseas. (8) We suffer a credibility gap in missions unless we find solutions to division at home. (9) To avoid the "brain drain," we should foster advanced education of nationals in their own countries.

6. Leadership

Issues: (1) What is the authentic role of the pastor? (2) Do we need a more structured approach to pastoral "placement?" (3) What is the rightful role of women in leadership? (4) What relationship exists between lay leadership development and the preparation of pastors? (5) What will be required of the leader in the new urban society? (6) Should the General Assembly agree on criteria for leadership? (7) What relation is there between leadership of the Holy Spirit and a reasoned, even structured approach to leadership development and deployment?

Consensus: (1) Pastoral leadership is crucial if competent laymen are to be actively involved in God's work. (2) There is a shortage of pastoral leadership, not quantitative but qualitative. (3) Ministerial drop-out is a serious problem. We need an effective support system for pastors. (4) There should be some youth representation on the Executive Council. (5) Leadership by the Holy Spirit mixes with human understanding and rational processes. (6) The minister should be "married to the mission not to the church." (7) Members of credentials committees should be trained with a code developed for their work. (8) We must help the church to think in terms of ability, not color. (9) Youth should be encouraged to select freely those with whom they wish to associate regardless of racial differences.

The digest of reflections above indicates the very broad scope of the consultation as a whole, but also the sharper focus of work done in the six sections. Again, as following the 1963 congress, the findings were widely studied with many of the suggestions being put into effect directly by the various state and national agencies. Beyond that, the indirect influence upon all policy was very significant.

C. Yokefellow Statement

108. Yokefellow Statement

1974

Reprinted from the 1974 Annual Reports (Anderson, Ind.; Executive Council, 1974), 29-31.

The following persons, eighteen members of the Division of General Service and seven state coordinators, gathered at Yokefellow House in Richmond, Indiana, May 9-10, 1974, have given prayerful consideration to these specific objectives upon which we feel the attention and resources of the Church of God should be brought to bear in the immediate years leading up to our centennial celebration in 1980-81. We call for, and pledge ourselves to, objectives in the following areas:

96

IDENTITY

We affirm the reformational role of the Church of God movement and, in keeping with this affirmation, call the church to repentance, cleansing, and reconciliation—both among ourselves and toward God—to the end that we may reestablish and renew our covenant relationship with God and each other, restore the biblical root system of our heritage, and thus nourish those things that draw us together as a people on mission for God in today's rootless and fragmented world.

In order to accomplish this, we covenant together that we will stress through every available channel the crucial importance of responsible study and exposition of the Holy Scriptures in all of our preaching and teaching, and with particular emphasis upon the centrality of Jesus Christ in his body, the Church, and upon the fulfillment of his mission in the world.

RELATIONSHIPS

In keeping with the historical dedication of the Church of God movement to Christian unity, individual freedom, and brotherhood, we affirm the importance of the unity that exists among us. While recognizing individual creativity and initiative, we call for responsible commitment to the Church's total mission at every level of its life and work, from the local to the worldwide, as our supreme objective. In our united opinion, this objective calls for:

1. Complete obedience to Christ and his Word.
2. Recognition of the dignity and freedom of human personality.
3. Commitment to each other as members of the Body of Christ.
4. Loyalty to, and support of the church's institutions and programs which we have created together.
5. Openness to the continuing revelation of God's Spirit in our common life.

It is our belief that the New Testament sets forth the ideal that all Christians, operating in true humanity, should be able to learn from one another. We maintain, moreover the conviction that this movement represents a force of reformation leadership within Christendom with its emphasis on ecumenicity based on unity rather than on union. To this end, therefore, we encourage through every means possible the establishing and maintaining of work relationships with other like-minded groups on the national, state, and local levels.

MINISTRY

The major purposes of the Church of God movement, so far as its origin and continuing life are concerned, must be clarified sufficiently to strengthen our ministerial and lay leadership in their preaching and teaching roles, with particular emphasis in the following areas:

1. To be more creative to discover, train, deploy, and conserve leadership.
2. To initiate programs and processes that are biblically centered for understanding and addressing social ills and injustices.
3. To promote the Christian ministry as a viable, exciting vocation and insist upon quality training.
4. To challenge our finest young men and women to give themselves in ministry.
5. To develop support systems for clergy where ministers and/or members of their family can find adequate counsel during marital, financial, physical, emotional, or vocational stress.

In keeping with the purposes of the Church of God movement, we urge that doctrinal concepts be periodically reviewed for strengthening the church's convictions. We further urge that the motivating force for ministry be rediscovered in order that the Church of God may have purpose for continued being.

INTEGRATION

The Church by nature is one; therefore, the Church must continuously work its way through and beyond racial relationships to functional unity. It must be recognized and admitted, in doing this, that racists' attitudes are incompatible with the Christian gospel of oneness, brotherhood, and love. As we work toward functional and visible unity, the following objectives should be kept clearly in mind:

1. Continue to emphasize the positive things which are being done to include persons of different racial and cultural origins and backgrounds in the decision-making processes at all levels of the Church's life and work.
2. Increase dialogue among persons of all races and cultures with a view toward helping local congregations of the Church of God become more effective and inclusive in their evangelistic and missionary outreach programs in the homeland and abroad.
3. Encourage and make possible the enrollment and training of youth from minority and ethnic groups included within the membership of the Church of God in our church-related colleges.
4. Further explore the structuring of state, regional, and national organizations of the Church of God in order to more truly express the oneness of the Church in the fulfillment of its mission in the world.
5. Recognize that attitudes relating to race must always be interpreted in the light of the social environment and climate in which the Church carries forth its mission but without any compromise with the principles of the Christian gospel.

POLITY

We affirm and recognize that the local congregation is the primary unit of ministry and outreach for fulfilling the Church's mission in the world, the stabilizing of the home, and in alleviating the tensions that undermine society. In order to strengthen the local congregation, we urge:

1. Better leadership preparation at all levels.
2. Stronger emphasis on personal and group study of the Word of God as a complement to public proclamation.
3. Development of greater stewardship commitment by individuals and congregations.

We further plead for the development of more precise lines of responsibility, cooperation, and communication between the local, state and national organizations of the Church of God that will reflect our interdependent relationships. Some areas in which this could serve a useful purpose are as follows:

1. Providing for a greater degree of participatory democracy in the life and government of the Church.
2. Cooperative planning, programming, goal setting, and budgeting.
3. Congregational and ministerial certification and credentials.
4. Establishment of new congregations and agencies.

R. Eugene Sterner	Roscoe Snowden	Ronald Fowler
Milburn H. Miller	Helen Miller	Ron Naille
Robert H. Reardon	Lester Crose	Max R. Gaulke
Forest F. Carlson	Francis Jolliff	Carl Peterson
Jesse A. Barber	Alfred Brown	Marvin J. Hartman
B. Gale Hetrick	W. E. Reed	Clayton Perry
Harold Conrad	James W. Fair	Donald A. Courtney
T. Franklin Miller	E. Joe Gilliam	W. E. Reed, Director
Raymond S. Miller	Paul A. Tanner	

D. Dialogue I on Internal Unity

109. Dialogue I on Internal Unity

January 1981

The period 1980-1981 saw significant controversy in the life of the Church of God. To assist helpfully in bringing the most significant issues into focus and in bringing representatives of varying viewpoints into direct and prolonged discussion about these issues, the Board of Directors of the Executive Council convened a dialogue on internal unity. Present were thirty leaders invited because of their leadership roles in the national, state, and local ministries of the Church of God. The group decided upon its own agenda, choosing three major areas with the first, biblical inspiration and authority, receiving the most attention. The results of searching and intense discussion were mailed to all members of the General Assembly. They were as follows.

ISSUE 1: BIBLICAL

How can the Church of God more adequately understand our position on the authority, inspiration, and nature of the Bible?
—Where are we agreed in our view of Scripture?
—Where are we not yet agreed?
—How much diversity can we have and still maintain unity?

AFFIRMATIONS
WE ARE AGREED THAT:

1. The Bible is the inspired Word of God—the source of authority for Christians in faith, doctrine, and practice (2 Tim. 3:16, 17).
2. The Bible is fully trustworthy and without error in its revelation of the will of God concerning man in all things necessary to salvation and Christian living.
3. We must depend on the Holy Spirit's guidance in interpreting the Scriptures.
4. The individual and corporate study of the Bible is essential to effective discipleship and mission in the world today.
5. Our technical differences pertaining to Scripture in no way call into question our commitment to the authority of Scripture.
6. In our view of Scripture there are still areas where we hold divergent views. This does not jeopardize our fellowship or our Christian commitment.

ISSUE 2: STRUCTURAL

What form of structure and/or polity can best serve the Church of God as it moves into its second century as a reformation movement in such areas as:
—The selection of leaders to serve national corporations, state organizations, and local congregations?
—The establishing of channels of communication through which more adequate information can be shared with the General Assembly by those who serve in leadership positions and who are accountable to the Assembly?
—The place of lay persons in the decision-making processes of the church—nationally, state and local?

SOME RECOMMENDATIONS

1. That a study be made of General Assembly functions which include frequency, location of and duration of meetings; the nature and format of the agenda. (Consider dialogue need and rotation of location.)
2. That a review be made of the nature of accountability of boards and agencies, Executive Council and its subordinate units and related para-church groups, and to develop guidelines by which that accountability can be expressed to the General Assembly.
3. The study should involve widespread participation of the church at large.
4. Recommended to Board of Directors that it encourage the Committee on Long Range Planning to initiate a continuing process which will allow all ministers of the church to share their views regarding the costs and priorities of the several agencies.
5. Use state and regional meetings, and so on as settings for communication seminars (to inform how national agencies function and means of access to them).
6. To develop a design for prayer support groups for individual agency personnel and their work.
7. A serious concern is expressed that our colleges are essentially unrelated and competitive. Some initiative should be taken to speak to this major problem.

ISSUE 3: RELATIONAL

What kind of unity do we seek in regard to social and moral issues as we are confronted by the mandates of Scripture regarding these?

More specifically, are we seeking agreement of stance on the various contemporary social, moral and ethical issues?

(a) as a united voice of the church?
(b) as a common view of the world?
(c) as a common interpretation of Scripture?
(d) as a test of fellowship?
(e) as a measure of acceptability of leaders?

SOME RECOMMENDATIONS

1. We recommended the development of scholarly statements on crucial social issues confronting the church. These can be printed resources, tapes or video-tapes which can be used in church study groups. These should present the various sides so that persons can "think" through what their own stance is. Positions of respected Church of God leaders should be clearly stated.
2. Develop a pattern of bringing together the best minds from the diverse points of view to dialogue in depth on selected issues. Resulting information and conclusions could be used in preparation of resources for #1.
3. Explore ways in which existing meetings may be used to dialogue on

the crucial issues faced in ministry; i.e. General Assembly and ministers meetings.

4. Make a better effort to include the conservative voice in deliberations on social issues from which study resources and position papers may be produced.

E. Dialogue II on Internal Unity

110. Dialogue II on Internal Unity

December 1981

The General Assembly was kept well informed about the results of the second dialogue convened in December 1981 by the Executive Council. Dr. Paul A. Tanner, executive secretary of the council, reported to the Assembly that "issues of general interest did provide a free and open exchange of views, but there was no overriding issue as experienced in Dialogue I." The twenty-eight participants representing fourteen different states decided to discuss three subject areas. They came to the following points of consensus and recommendations.

ISSUE I

Priesthood of Believers
CONSENSUS
1. The Scripture does support an orderly process in the work of the Church, but does not prescribe a specific polity.
2. We believe in the priesthood of believers, but this concept does not determine the specific numerical composition of the General Assembly.
3. We value increased involvement of Spirit-gifted lay persons in the General Assembly of the Church of God and its various structures.
4. The present proposed model for increasing lay participation in the General Assembly will not likely be accepted by the Church.
RECOMMENDATIONS
1. That lay participation be selected from and by existing formal assemblies.
2. Unless the Bylaws Committee can come up with a proposal that gives greater evidence of acceptability, that they request a year's further study.

ISSUE II

Leadership Development in Higher Education
CONSENSUS

102

1. We have a genuine appreciation for the richness and diversity among our institutions of higher education and express concerns only out of a sense of stewardship for these resources.
2. We sense a great deal of frustration among ourselves over the competition and independency of action on the part of our educational institutions and other problems relating to the need for overall coordination and supervision of our higher educational process.

RECOMMENDATION

That the Board of Directors of the Executive Council appoint a committee to study ways similar communions structure their institutions of higher education and make recommendations for the corporate structuring of our approach to higher education.

ISSUE III

Church of God Response to World Issues
CONSENSUS

The Church of God has a biblical mandate to be involved in world issues by caring and doing.

RECOMMENDATIONS

1. Need to cultivate greater awareness of what is being done and should be done, by focusing on these in church publications and news media.
2. Upgrade image and work of Commission on Social Concerns by changing the name and assure the membership to be more inclusive (not only those of vested or concentrated interest) to increase its effectiveness.
3. Suggest that the 1983 International Convention Program Committee develop a theme emphasis to speak to a response to world issues, with speakers who can/will focus on the positive, evangelical Kingdom—now.
4. Suggest that the editor of *Vital Christianity* consider an issue with the theme of Church of God World Responsibility in the areas listed.

F. Consultation on Mission and Ministry

111. Consultation on Mission and Ministry

1984

An intensive study and evaluation of the structure and function of the Executive Council was commissioned during the mid-1970s. Among the issues that emerged in that study was one expressing the need for the

Church of God to be involved in long-range planning in a more aggressive and coordinated way. Up until that time the only instance of coordinated effort at long-range planning at the national level was lodged with the Division of General Service. Restructuring was decided on and included the termination of the Division of General Service and the formation of the Committee on Long Range Planning.

Very early in its work the committee established its own priorities. It quickly recognized that it could not, on its own, formulate goals for the work of the church. This recognition gave rise to the idea of a national consultation that would be broadly representative of the total church in all of its diversity. Initial approval for such a consultation was given by the Executive Council in May 1982.

One hundred and thirty-five selected Church of God leaders from across the United States and Canada convened in Indianapolis on April 2-5, 1984, for four days of provocative and stimulating dialogue. The event was identified as a major Consultation on Mission and Ministry. It was the most representative and ambitious attempt of its kind in Church of God history. What follows is a brief summary of the central concerns and goals projected by this consultation for the Church of God to the end of this century.

AREA I

Concern: Truth—Here We Stand!

Purpose: To affirm the biblical foundations for the mission and ministry of the church and highlight central biblical teachings.

Goal: To establish the Bible as the authority for the faith and life of the church.

We live in a time when traditional authority is questioned and an increasing number of persons, even in the church, are biblically illiterate. The Bible must be accepted as authoritative in the church and its contents must be taught and preached with clarity, discipline, and integrity.

Goal: To witness to those biblical truths central to the particular mission of the Church of God movement.

The effectiveness of the ministry of the Church of God depends heavily on its own understanding of its distinctive mission as a particular fellowship and movement among God's people. The biblical truths central to this distinctive mission must be clarified, taught, and lived out.

Goal: To understand the church as a covenant community called to servanthood.

The church today lives in an unstable and materialistic society. To be a faithful, influential and relevant witness in the world, the church must become a covenant community dedicated to the service of persons for the sake of Christ. This will require a biblical understanding of covenant and servanthood. It also will require sacrifice, even suffering.

AREA II

Concern: Into All the World

Purpose: To broaden the church's understanding of world concerns and to motivate the church to fulfill its mission and ministry in the world. It is possible for the church to live in the world, but remain aloof and "not a part of the world." The church is called to act within the world but not let the world squeeze it into its mold. Let the church be the church—the model of ministry, care, and concern guided by its understanding of the world in which it lives and works.

Goal: To work toward global awareness and to recognize our responsibility to the whole world in Christian action and concern for world issues.

Goal: To sensitize the Church of God to the cultural distinctives of all persons in our world and to affirm their God-given dignity.

Goal: To become involved as the people of God who work for change at those points where the gospel speaks to the world in which we live.

AREA III

Concern: Mission—Good News!

Purpose: To understand the mission of the church to present the gospel to every person through the power of the Holy Spirit at work in us.

Goal: To develop a statement of the mission of the Church of God Reformation Movement.

The Church of God has always been a people on mission, a people with a purpose. As we seek to clarify our own understanding of our unique message and mission, state it forthrightly and communicate it to others, we will be able to live it out more effectively.

Goal: To equip persons to evangelize, nurture, and bring to maturity all persons who are lost from God and separated from one another. As we become more sensitive to the many ways persons are separated from God and each other, we will become increasingly motivated to lead them to Christ. In response to the Great Commission we will go out in the power of the Holy Spirit to make disciples. We will continue to teach and equip one another for this task.

Goal: To challenge the Church of God to redemptive action in relation to the social issues of our time.

To serve Christ is to serve in the arena of human need. Our ministry of reconciliation must take us into the middle of the world's problems with redemptive action. We will respond to Christ's call to "preach good news to the poor . . . proclaim release to the captives and recovering of sight to the blind, to set at liberty those who are oppressed!" (Luke 4:18)

AREA IV

Concern: A Living Church

Purpose: To live out a ministry that fulfills the mission of the church as the people of God.

Goal: To prize the family as the basic unit in God's design for human relationships.

The family, vital to every person's fulfillment, is an endangered species. Fast-paced living is emptying homes, making them temporary storage places and little more. But the family is of God's design, and we are stewards of this resource. The Church must help families to live in wholeness.

Goal: To strengthen the competence and effectiveness of ministerial leadership in the church.

The care and feeding of leaders is essential to the living church. Many, however, are crippled in effectiveness, wounded in the line of duty, unprepared, undisciplined for the challenges of a changing world. The church must offer the guidance and support to heal our healers.

Goal: To understand the biblical foundations for accountability and inclusiveness in ministry.

Congregational freedom has not offered redemptive or useful ways to bring accountability to ministry. Conflicts often become diseases of destruction rather than building blocks for new strength. Women are being called, trained, ordained for ministry, but few are called to local pastorates.

Goal: To inspire all believers to use their gifts in the ministry of the church.

Preparation and call of lay persons to a ministry of the common life is needed to release some of God's best, but least discovered, resources for ministry. Lay muscles will mobilize the church.

Goal: To mobilize the church to implement the national strategy for church planting as adopted by the General Assembly, June 1984.

A surge of renewal for the movement will happen as we plant new churches. Seven hundred and seventy-three new congregations in ten years is a goal which can revitalize the movement, but only by a massive strategy of cooperation. The involvement of everyone is needed to achieve such a goal.

AREA V

Concern: Being the Body of Christ

Purpose: To develop mutually interdependent relationships that enable the church to be effective in fulfilling its mission and ministry within the whole body of Christ.

Goal:	To affirm the value and to strengthen the practice of interdependence within the Church of God.

Throughout our history we have experienced a growing understanding of the importance of interdependence to the successful achievement of our goals. For both practical and theological reasons we know that "we really do need each other."

Goal:	To determine and develop the best structures that best express interdependence and enable ministry and mission in the Church of God throughout the world.

There is always more than one way to get a job done. Throughout our history we have sought to be sensitive to the Holy Spirit and responsive to the needs in creating structures to do the work of the church.

We will continue to create structures that reflect our need for interdependence.

Goal:	To establish specific time-related goals to be implemented through the church's interdependent structures.

We increasingly sense the need for setting specific goals for implementing our mission and ministry. For the goals to have meaning they must be the result of the widest possible involvement of the church at all levels. We sense a special call to give attention to growth and evangelism goals.

Goal:	To expand ministries through voluntary relationships with church groups outside the Church of God Reformation Movement.

Our quest for Christian unity brings us into relationships with all members of the Body of Christ. Through voluntary relationships we can often achieve our mission more effectively and expand our ministries.

Goal:	To lift up the responsibility of every congregation for ministry to the whole world, affirming our interdependence in recognition of the enormity of the task of global evangelization.

The task of global evangelization is enormous. The common mission we share calls us to live out our Christian unity and to experience interdependence as we seek to fulfill our common discipleship in the world.

112. Glossolalia

June 1986

During the 1985 General Assembly of the Church of God a resolution was presented from the General Assembly of Ohio. It called for the establishment of a study committee "composed of qualified individuals from the academic and pastoral fields to study the work of the Holy Spirit as related to glossolalia in light of Scripture, our historical perspective and present happenings in the Church of God movement." The resolution was referred to the Executive Council through which a study committee was named. In June, 1986, the committee submitted an extensive report. The Assembly received it with appreciation and commended "for careful study and guidance throughout the Church of God the biblical guidelines, observations and recommendations contained in this report." In part they were as follows.

With particular reference to the gift of tongues, the following are understood to be biblical guidelines for its definition and exercise:

A. A gift of tongues is listed in the New Testament as one of the gifts which a given believer might receive as God chooses. Defining and governing the exercise of such a potential gift are important and difficult tasks in the context of the life of the contemporary church and in light of the limited Biblcal teaching on the subject.

B. A gift of tongues, however defined, is not given to all Spirit-filled believers (1 Cor. 12:28-30) and is not the evidence of the infilling of the Holy Spirit. Paul's discussion of evidence, as seen in 1 Corinthians, chapters 12-14, clearly states that a life of love is the essential evidence. Chapter 14 must be understood in the context of chapters 12 and 13, particularly 1 Cor. 12:1-3 and chapter 13.

C. Which gift or how many gifts a person is given is not a factor in that person's salvation or sanctification. What is a factor is the reception of the Gift, that of the Holy Spirit (Act 1:8 and Romans 8:9). A gift of tongues, therefore, should not be regarded as proof of spirituality on the part of the speaker. Any insistence to the contrary lies outside biblical teaching and leads easily to distortion in the meaning and intended use of spiritual gifts.

D. A gift of tongues, according to the instances recorded in Acts, probably was the supernaturally-given ability to speak in human languages not previously learned by the speaker. If so defined, the purpose of this gift was (1) to provide a tool for the multilingual proclamation of the gospel and/or (2) to provide a sign of the universal nature of the Christian faith.

E. A gift of tongues, according to the teaching in 1 Corinthians, is less clear in its nature. While it could have been a deterioration of the phenomenon of tongues at pentecost or an extreme emotionalism related to local pagan practices, it may well have been a gift to some Christians of the ability to speak in the presence of God, which speaking required interpretation in public worship (1 Cor. 14:2). Whatever its nature, its manifestations in Corinth involved a range of problems which called for strict pastoral discipline. The problems centered in wrong personal attitudes, a misunderstanding of spiritual gifts and unacceptable public practices. These problems were addressed by the Apostle Paul in part through the giving of the following guidelines:

1. Unintelligible speech in public worship is unacceptable (1 Cor. 14:9).

2. A gift of tongues should be seen as the least of the gifts because the person who so speaks without interpretation (unless in

private) addresses God and does not directly edify the church through exercising the gift. A gift like prophecy, the ability to communicate clearly the word of God, is to be valued as a greater gift (1 Cor. 14:1-12, 19).

3. A gift of tongues should not violate the assumption that Christian worship services should be characterized by dignity, orderliness and self-control (I Cor. 14:23, 32, 40).

4. A gift of tongues, if exercised in a public service, requires the presence and exercise of another gift, the gift of interpretation. Because the purpose of spiritual gifts is the upbuilding of the church, this latter gift is needed to bring the former back into the realm of common understanding and edification. If a gift of tongues is exercised publicly, it is to be governed by the following (1 Cor. 14:26-32):

   a. Only two or three persons may so speak in one service.
   b. Never should more than one person speak at the same time.
   c. Someone must always interpret the speaking or it is not appropriate to proceed.
   d. There should be no confusion, only decency, order and edification.

The following are offered as biblical guidelines for local church life:

1. Local congregations of the Church of God are urged to give careful attention to acquainting persons with the traditional beliefs and practices of the Church of God regarding glossolalia (particularly the biblical guidelines stated above).

2. Congregations also are urged to teach the central importance of the work of the Holy Spirit in the lives of believers and in the process of genuine Christian worship.

3. Corporate authority over individualistic assertiveness in congregational life is vital. Submission to each other in the Spirit of Christ is a key to harmonious church life.

4. Persons who feel that it is important to promote private manifestations and/or public demonstrations of a gift of tongues in violation of Biblical guidelines should not expect leadership positions in Church of God congregations.

5. Any proposal for major change in a congregation's worship style or practices should be implemented with sensitivity to the whole congregation and not merely in response to the preference of a few, including the pastor. Congregations contemplating such a major change might well seek counsel first from respected Church of God leaders outside the congregation.

6. While not wishing to build walls between Christians, serious concern is expressed about the negative effects on local congregations coming from well-financed Christian groups promoting charismatic concepts and practices opposed to the Biblical guidelines stated above.

113. Task Force on Governance and Polity

1987-1991

The Task Force on Governance and Polity was established by the June, 1987, General Assembly and given the charge "to undertake a wideranging analysis of present governance and polity traditions, assumptions, structures, and relationships; to develop recommendations for enhancing the effectiveness of governance and polity—congregational, state and national—to the end that mission and ministry are strengthened." The assignment became one of five years, with substantive progress reports to the assembly annually. The fourth report was given in June, 1991. It detailed "emerging priorities" and identified as a basic issue "the tension between authority and autonomy." While the final report would come in 1992, the 1991 report presented five recommendations, all of which were approved by the Assembly. These follow.

1. Expanded Lay Membership in the General Assembly.
We recommend that all categories of present membership . . . be maintained. . . . We further recommend that the following persons who are properly named and present in any meeting shall be members of the Assembly, effective with the General Assembly of 1993:
—one layperson from each congregation, AM attendance to 100;
—two laypersons from each congregation, AM attendance to 500;
—three laypersons from each congregation, AM attendance to 1,000;
—four laypersons from each congregation, AM attendance over 1,001.
We further recommend that this action receive a full evaluation and after three years of operation, with the Executive Council directed to design and conduct the evaluation, recommend action related to continuation, and bring that recommendation to the 1996 General Assembly for ratification.
2. Establishment of a Mission and Ministry Triennial.
We accept the general recommendation . . . regarding establishing a Mission and Ministry Triennial . . . and request the Task Force to develop further details and projections in its 1992 report.
3. Expectations of the Executive Council.
   1. Act as the central corporate body for envisioning church-wide direction, formulating goals, and initiating follow-up to established directions and goals.
   2. Be the central coordinative body for national ministries of the Church.
   3. Provide a viable and strengthened linkage between national and state ministries.
   4. Call national agencies to accountability with respect to those directions and goals which the General Assembly or Executive Council has approved or established.
   5. Oversee the performance and management of the legal, administrative and financial responsibilities of the Council in its relationships

with the national agencies, national and international conventions and other segments of the work of the Church of God.
4. Executive Council: Membership, Name, Meetings.
(Tentative thinking on changes in the council's membership, name and meeting time were presented. The Assembly concurred in general and asked for definitive recommendations by 1992.)
5. Renewal Among National Corporations.
We recommend that the following take place in 1991-92:
—That the Task Force continue to nurture constructive dialogue among representatives (staff and boards) of these national corporations; and
—That the Executive Secretary of the Executive Council, within the spirit of the earlier recommendations concerning that office, initiate fresh cooperative consultations among the national corporations, built around the service clusters listed above; that new programming be cleared through these consultations.

114. Mission of the Church of God

June 1988

The mission of the Church of God is to be a caring community of God's covenant people under the Lordship of Jesus Christ and the leadership of the Holy Spirit:
—To proclaim the love of God, through Jesus Christ, to all persons;
—To enable persons throughout all the world to experience redemptive love in its fullest meaning through the sanctifying power of the Gospel and know Jesus Christ as Savior, Master, and Lord;
—To call persons to holiness and discipleship;
—To equip persons to be servants of Christ in the world;
—To live as citizens of the Kingdom of God here and now, work for justice, mercy and peace, and abide in the Christian hope;
—To build up the whole body of Christ in unity.

Editor's note: This statement was developed by the Committee on Long Range Planning, then endorsed by the Executive Council and General Assembly and "commended to the Church as a resource and working document in the pursuit of its multi-faceted ministries."

115. Open Forum with Christian Churches/Churches of Christ

1989-1991

Beginning in 1989 the Commission on Christian Unity of the Church of God joined with leaders of the Christian Churches/Churches of Christ to sponsor an ongoing series of annual open forums. The general purpose was a disciplined dialogue between two fellowships with much in common. With no thought of merger as a possible outcome, efforts were directed toward building acquaintance, encouraging Christian fellowship and nurturing true Christian unity in the Spirit. Scholars from each group met in August 1991, to explore in depth several doctrines that traditionally were assumed either to unite or divide these fellowships. Increasing ways are being explored to broaden these conversations, even to include some cooperative ministry opportunities. The General Assembly of the Church of God was kept informed of progress in this evolving relationship.

Section IV

Questions for the Future

A. Role of the General Assembly

B. Style of the General Assembly

C. Membership of the General Assembly

D. Meetings of the General Assembly

E. Agenda of the General Assembly

Questions for the Future

The year 1980 saw the reformation movement of the Church of God celebrate its first century of ministry. Much has changed and much has been accomplished over these many years. The General Assembly has acted often to create, encourage, and direct new forms of ministry at the national level. As is obvious from the preceding pages, it also has spoken its conviction on a wide range of crucial issues that have faced the Church of God and society at large.

Now is a good time to review the process and implications of all of this activity and to think carefully about the future of the Assembly. Given all the material in this book about the nature and actions of the Assembly in the past, let us look to tomorrow.

A. Role of the General Assembly. In light of the historic stance of the Church of God against the dangers of denominationalism, the assembly has been careful to call itself "voluntary" and to deny itself "ecclesiastical authority." But there always is pressure for some influential and concerned person or body to clarify a teaching which is in question or to bind an organization of the church to the consensus thinking of the church. It is easy for some persons, lacking any effective alternative, to look to the assembly for such clarification or binding. Should the assembly continue to resist assuming such authoritative roles? Would the integrity of the reformation movement be compromised if the assembly would assume such roles? Should the assembly speak to or for the church—or should it speak at all on controversial issues? How can the assembly better avoid becoming the stage on which attempts are made to circumvent the legally vested governance functions of the several national agencies?

B. Style of the General Assembly. Some annual meetings of the assembly, reflecting a period of turmoil in the church, have been characterized by the presence of tension and heated debate. The 1981 report to the assembly by the executive secretary of the Executive Council, for instance, expressed concern over the "recent politicizing of our General Assembly. To coalesce and muster persons to come with a block vote seems more the ways of man and less the leading of the Holy Spirit." Will the assembly become increasingly like the conventions of national political parties, trying to hammer out a platform, or can it retain an orderly and trusting atmosphere in which all persons function as humble servants of God and not as persons maneuvering for some political advantage? Is the Church of God really different from other church bodies in the way it does its business? In what way should and can it be different?

C. Membership of the General Assembly. The assembly began as a fellowship meeting of ministers. Its first formal action in 1917 stated that only ordained ministers of the Church of God could vote. Through the years, however, there has been much discussion about appropriate membership guidelines. Should the assembly be delegated, not because of a desire to restrict the participation of ministers, but because geography has seemed to limit the participation of some ministers, giving the ministers of some states a disproportionate representation? [If not delegated, should the assembly rotate its meeting locations or find some means of funding travel costs so that all ministers have an equal opportunity to participate?] And what about the role of laypersons? An increased number now are included, but many ministers and laypersons feel that the theology of the church calls for a large increase in lay involvement. What is appropriate? What are the possible advantages and practical problems related to increasing lay membership in the Assembly?

D. Meetings of the General Assembly. As the organized ministries of the church have grown in number and complexity over the years, the assembly has assumed more business functions. Reports, ratifications, ballots, budgets, and resolutions have come to use most available time. The sheer size of the assembly now necessitates considerable formality and the few hours of meeting time each year are sandwiched among the scores of events of the International Convention. Serious group prayer, in-depth exploration of issues, and careful long-range planning have become difficult in this setting. Should, therefore, assembly meetings convene in groups for longer periods rather than in the assembly itself? Should assembly sessions be at a time other than during the International Convention which is held annually in June in Anderson, Indiana? Apparently, these questions will be answered in part in the future by the periodic convening of a Mission and Ministry Triennial, a concept approved by the 1991 General Assembly (see entry 113).

E. Agenda of the General Assembly. Recent years have seen a growing parade of resolutions on subjects of concern to one group or another in the assembly. It has been assumed that such formal statements by the assembly are appropriate and meaningful actions. Should this practice of making pronouncements on a variety of timely subjects continue to be a preoccupation of the assembly? How accessible should the floor of the assembly be to the concerns of small groups within its membership? Regarding the stating of "general reformation principles" (see entries 25-27), where is the line between declaring appropriately the central truths that make us the people of God and acting inappropriately by establishing creedal positions and building denominational fences?